Dear Julie –

It's always hard to buy you a present but I know that you love books. I also know that you didn't have any on Chinese Art.

Hope you enjoy this one !!!

Love, Bob (Xmas 1984)

THE
PERFECT
UNION

THE
PERFECT
UNION

THE CHINESE METHODS

Text by
ANTOINE DENIS

Crescent Books

New York

Crédits : Institute for Sex Research (Indiana University) : 2, 5, 7, 11, 12, 13, 20, 21, 23, 24, 25, 29, 52 — Gichner Foundation : 9, 17, 41, 46, 57, 64, 70 — Pr Mandel : 31, 32, 33, 35, 36, 37, 38, 40, 42, 43, 44, 45, 48, 49, 54, 55, 59, 60, 62, 63, 65, 66, 67, 73, 74, 75, 76, 77, 79.

Designed and produced by
Productions Liber SA

First English edition published by
Productions Liber SA

© Productions Liber SA
Fribourg - Genève, 1984

ISBN 0-517-44805X

This edition is published by Crescent Books.
Distributed by Crown Publishers, Inc.

h g f e d c b a

Printed in Italy

Never have the Chinese had an attitude which could in any way be described as pornographic in relation to erotic texts and pictures. Not that this has prevented them, during the different periods of their history, from drawing up an infinite number of methods, with no lack of illustrations, intended to initiate not only men but also women into the secrets of love and sex. For scholars, poets and doctors throughout Chinese history, making love in the best possible conditions was necessary for physical and mental health, and the art of love was an essential part of the natural order of things; it helped to prolong life. It was an integral part of the Taoist philosophy, thanks to which Ancient China lived completely free of sexual repression and the abnormalities that other ancient civilizations had the misfortune to suffer.

The present century has discovered, not without a certain surprise, some of the secrets of the sexual relations of the ancient Taoists. Certain of their precepts seem rather revolutionary even in our time; for example, the assertion that a man's orgasm and his ejaculation are not one and the same thing. In the Taoist art of love, medicine combines with pleasure and wisdom, so that love and sex can really be of great benefit to the human being; which is, of course, only possible if there is total satisfaction on the part of the two partners of the couple.

The word "Tao" means, in fact, "reason"; it represents popular wisdom, which began to develop thousands years ago. In the 6th century B.C., the poet Lao-Tsen gathered together his beliefs, his philosophy and the popular practices in vogue at the time, in the *Tao Tê Ching*, or the *"Book of Tao"*, which represents the very base on which Taoism is founded. It is a comparatively short book, but of prime importance for the Chinese people. According to the Tao, man only has his place in the organization of the universe as an insignificant and vulnerable creature. He must, therefore, make a great effort to live in harmony with the sources of nature. To practise the Tao, then, it is necessary to be natural, careful and calm, in order to become part of the strength and energy of the cosmos.

THE YIN AND THE YANG – THE MANUALS

The long history of China has seen conflicts arise between Confucianism and Taoism. Confucius and his practical philosophy proved to be an efficient instrument for governing the country as well as organizing society and establishing family life, based on a patriarchal system. Taoism, for its part, was the living expression of the very deeply-felt pagan romanticism of the Chinese, and it stood out against the effectiveness of the methods of established government. The contradiction arising from these two beliefs was solved in all simplicity by the Ancient Chinese: the head just had to follow the precepts of Confucianism while the heart remained faithful to Taoism.

The three basic concepts of the Tao in relation to sex are, first of all, that man must learn to find an interval before ejaculation which is suitable, bearing in mind the man's age and his physical condition, then that the ejaculation is not the moment when the man necessarily reaches the climax of ecstasy, and that there are numerous ways for him to take pleasure in sex, and lastly, that the satisfaction of the woman is also of great importance.

These three basic concepts cannot possibly be imagined without taking into account the necessary harmony between the *yin* and the *yang,* two words which represent the very essence of the Tao, the *yin* representing the female and the *yang* the male. These two terms have also been used to mean cosmic forces which complete each other, such as the earth and the heavens, the moon and the sun, forces that perpetuate the universe in an eternal cycle. The origin of these two complementary characters is not really known, but it is known that in more recent times, they began to be described by a classic design, the *yin* indicating the region south of a river and the north slope of a hill, and the *yang* the north bank of a river and the south side of a hill.

Relations between the sexes are both the foundation of universal life and a demonstration of complementary cosmic forces. According to the book *Yi-king,* which is not only a practical manual of divination but also a philosophical treatise: "The constant intermingling of the Earth and the Sky gives a shape to everything. The sexual union between a man and a woman gives life to everything." This book refers also to man and woman by the *yin* and the *yang.* To reach a perfect, healthy sexual life, it is necessary to harmonize the lines of the *yin* and the *yang,* which, according to the Ancient Chinese were six in number: the first three, called *K'an,* represent *water, clouds* and *woman,* while the bottom three lines, called *li,* symbolize *fire, light* and *man.*

According to the great specialist on the matter, Robert van Gulik: "All the manuals about sex speculate about the different aspects of this hexagramme:... the element "woman" occupies the upper part of the Hexagramme (...) in the binominal *yin-yang,* and *yin* always comes first. We have perhaps there", adds the specialist, "the remains of the emotional reactions of the matriarchy." Then, further on: "As for the elements 'fire' and 'water', it can be noticed that medical treatises and works devoted to sex describe the sexual experience of a

man by comparing it to fire while a woman's is compared with water. Fire easily and quickly bursts into flame, but it dies down just as easily under the effect of water; on the other hand, water takes a long time to heat, but it also takes a longer time to cool down.

For almost three centuries, from 618 to 907, China was governed by the T'ang dynasty, which produced twenty-two sovereigns. It was during this period that arts and sciences reached their zenith, and it was also at this time that manuals about sex became commonplace and easily laid hands on, manuals that, even if they did originally have an author, were nothing like ordinary individual works. The man who was responsible for them, in fact, did nothing but content himself with gathering together various very ancient texts, to which he added customs handed down by oral tradition, as well as medical information. All of this, moreover, he put into verse.

In general, these works contained six chapters or sections, which were distinctly separate one from the other. They started with an introduction about the cosmic significance of the sexual union and its beneficial consequences for the health of the two partners. Then the book continued with a description of all the preliminaries to the sexual act, followed by a definition of the sexual act itself, and details of the various positions suitable for performing the act in. The fifth part dealt with the therapeutic aspect of sexual union, and the book concluded with a few pieces of advice and miscellaneous hints.

All these books were circulated in the form of manuscripts, with all the risks that this involved, the possibility of parts of them being lost or of corrections and variations being added.

From 982 to 984 a Japanese doctor of Chinese origin, called Tamba Yasuyori, took upon himself the task of collecting together hundreds of books and fragments of different works, in short, everything that he could find in the way of compilations of ideas on medical science, manuals about sex, books of prescriptions etc... Then he himself composed a work from all this in thirty parts, a real encyclopaedia, which he called *Yi-hsing-fang*.

The twenty-eighth part of this vast and comprehensive study, entitled *Fang-nei* ("the bedroom") includes fragments of five sexual manuals from Ancient China. It was by basing his research on this part of Tamba Yasuyori's work that, at the beginning of the present century, the Chinese writer Ye Tö-hoei managed to reconstitute the original texts which he had published in 1914. Among them was the famous *Tong-hsuan-tze* or "The Art of Love by the Master Tong-hsuan", a scholar who was principal of the Medical School during the 7th century. It is through this work of Ye Tö-hoei's that the Western World knows today about the sexual characteristics and the contents of the Ancient Chinese works. The initiative taken by Ye Tö-hoei, however, deeply shocked the men of letters of his time, and the publication of the five sexual manuals on the customs of the T'ang period ruined his career as a writer. He was shunned and died in 1927, after having been attacked by bandits.

THE SEXUAL ACT, SOURCE OF STRENGTH AND LONGEVITY

In his work, Tong-hsuang speaks of the human as being the most precious element in Creation, and nothing in man's life can be compared with the sexual act. The carnal relationship makes it possible to harmonize the *yin* and the *yang,* to nourish man's nature and to make life last for long and enjoyable years. As for those who do not follow the advice or accept the indications given for ensuring the best conditions for the sexual act and thus bringing about their complete fulfilment, they will die early and in misery.

All the sexual manuals emphasize repeatedly the advice that a man should make love with several different women in the course of one single night. This is not, however, an incitement to debauchery, even if it is not an encouragement of a simple marital relationship either. In Ancient China, in fact, the family was polygamous. And so it is that the manuals always allude to relationships which come within the normal order of things. A well-established businessman could have three or four wives, and the higher one rose in the social hierarchy, the higher too rose the number of wives. Princes and great generals sometimes had as many as

To give more strength to his companion, the man will lie on his back... The act should be performed in this way ten days running.'

thirty or more, and the change of partner then corresponded with a real need. It was not really a question of health but rather a desire to maintain a fine balance in the family, since favouritism could cause quarrels, jealousy and even hatred amongst the women who lived under the same roof. If the sexual manuals always refer to the happiness of the man, they do also speak of the happiness of his wives. On this point, they often advise the man to do his utmost to understand the behaviour and the sexual needs of his wives. And the two partners must, in any case, reach a perfect emotional harmony in order to be able to be sexually united.

The woman is of prime importance in this kind of work, often written in the form of a dialogue. It is they who most often play the role of initiator and give their partners information on the subject of the sexual act. It was considered to be essential that the woman should reach an orgasm during each union. And this gave rise to very detailed descriptions which made it possible to observe one's partner closely and to bring her to a state of total enjoyment.

In an extract from the book *Son-nu-king,* for example, which was later taken up again by the *Yi-hsing-fang,* the Yellow Emperor complains to the daughter of Candour that he is sad and fearful, and that he feels a certain weakness and lacks physical harmony. And the woman replies that when the man feels himself getting weaker, he must realize that this is because he is not performing the sexual act in the proper way. For in the same way as water is stronger than fire, so woman is superior to man. It is absolutely necessary for the two partners to be in

"The man and the woman shall not forget that complaints caused by the sexual act can also be cured by it."

complete accord in the sexual act, just as good cooks succeed in combining the five aromas perfectly in order to make a tasty dish of them. Those who have mastered the art of the *yin* and the *yang* know how to combine the five pleasures, but the others will die without having taken their full pleasure from love and sex. A man can reach an advanced age, using his semen sparingly, thanks to an appropriate diet and the use of different drugs, but of what use is this if he does not master the methods of sexual practices? The man and the woman, when they copulate, recall the meeting of the Heavens and the Earth. It is a question of two "acts" which, if they are carried out correctly, will last for ever. Man would be immortal if he could manage to stop the waning of his powers and to cure his illnesses by the *yin* and the *yang*. For the Ancient Chinese, it was a matter of becoming familiar with the Tao disciplines and, when the man visited his harem, the essential thing for him to do was to copulate often with very young women, ejaculating as little as possible, "so that his body might become light and free from all kinds of disease".

In the same passage, one of the Emperor's servants adds that the "secret of the Bedroom" lies in the *yin* and the *yang*. If one wants to prolong one's life, one must seek its source. In order to do this, it is better not to take undue advantage of the presence of very beautiful women, for they will bring one too easily to the point of ejaculation, and too great a flow of semen tires the veins and blood-vessels and, as a result, allows "hundreds of diseases" to make their way into the body. The ordinary man has only one wife, and this may well be enough to cause his downfall! For the man who knows all the secrets of the sexual

relationship, the greatest problem is to manage to find a sufficiently large number of women with whom to copulate. It does not matter at all whether they are beautiful and attractive or not, provided that they are young and plump. A man should have a minimum of seven or eight at his disposal, because if he always copulates with the same woman, his vital essence weakens, he becomes thin and can no longer transmit his "benefits" to his fellows. What is best for him is to copulate with more than ten women in one single night.

The Yellow Emperor then asks why it is that the woman seems never to be content with the act of copulation and is not roused to excitement, while the Jade Stem of the man does not become erect at all but remains small and listless.

This time, it is the Girl with Jet-black Hair who gives him his answer. She explains to him that when the woman wants to copulate and the man is thinking of other things, or when the man is eager for the sexual act but the woman shows no enthusiasm for it, this means that their hearts are lacking in harmony and that their vital essence cannot be activated. The *yin* then has to suffer the influence of the *yang* and vice versa. "But", replied the Emperor, "when at the moment of making love my Jade Stem does not become erect, I blush with shame, and beads of sweat fall from my brow. However, as I keenly want to copulate, I briskly rub my member with my hand".

"This is a painful experience common to all men," answers the Girl, "it must never be forgotten that when one wants to have a sexual relationship with a woman, it is very important to maintain a well-established order. In the first place, and this is indispensable, the two partners must harmonize their states of mind. First of all, they will engage in a long and pleasant conversation with each other, so that their sentiments may be united well before their bodies. After this, the man will be able to introduce his member into the woman, even if it is not yet rigid, and to withdraw it, even if it is very hard. In any case, these movements of introduction and withdrawal will be carried out very slowly. And during the coition, the man will avoid the emission of his semen. If he manages to copulate a number of times during one single night, and to avoid ejaculating, his ills will disappear and the duration of his life will be prolonged."

"What would be the consequences", continues the Emperor of China, "that would have to be suffered by a man who decided to abstain completely from any sexual relationship?" It is then that the daughter of Candour explains to him that the consequences could be nothing but bad, since the Heavens and the Earth would have closed within themselves. The spirit of the man would no longer be able to develop normally, because there would be a split between the *yin* and the *yang*. The repeated act of sharing which takes place at the time of sexual intercourse, makes it possible to mix the vital essence of the man with that of the woman, and produces a continual renewal, which can be nothing but beneficial. Death can be the final consequence of the inactivity of the Jade Stem.

In the book of *Yu-fang-pi-kine,* the Yellow Emperor asks some new questions. He wants to know, for example, how one can know if a girl reaches an orgasm. The reply is as follows: "First of all the woman's face goes very red and she clenches her fists with the palms turned downwards. It is then that the man can begin to kiss her tenderly; shortly afterwards, the tips

"They could see a certain number of advantages in the fact that there were such differences in age. Thus, when the man was more mature, he had his erection more slowly... The relationships between an older woman and a young man can also offer advantages for the two partners."

of her breasts harden, and she begins to sigh deeply. Thirdly, she turns up her palms and begins to play with the man's body, her throat becomes dry and she has difficulty in swallowing her saliva. She begins then to rock the lower part of her body backwards and forwards, and she closes her eyes. Fifthly, her vagina becomes moist and her throat utters a series of small sounds. It is now certain that the right moment for penetration has arrived. To these five signs can be added the five desires which enable one to judge the reactions of a woman. First of all, her respiration becomes irregular when she thinks with pleasure of the possibility of coition. Then her mouth and her nostrils will open slightly, as her external sexual organs are aroused to a real desire for union. In the third place, she will begin little movements of her body, from top to bottom, intended to activate her vital essence. Then a liquid will flow from her vagina and will wet her legs and her clothes. It is from this that one will see that her desire needs to be satisfied. Lastly, she will close her eyes, and her body, at the moment of reaching an orgasm, will become completely rigid.

One can count, moreover, ten sorts of movements of the woman's body during the sexual act. First of all, to show her desire for sexual union, she clasps the man's body close to her with her two arms. Second, she stretches out her legs to invite him to stimulate her clitoris. Third, she shows by the movements of her abdomen that she wants him to give her gentle little thrusts. Fourth, she begins to move her buttocks to show that she is experiencing pleasure. Fifth, she raises her legs to show her desire for harder thrusts. Sixth, she closes her thighs tightly together at the moment when she releases her fluid. Seventh, she lets her desire to be penetrated be made known, by means of slight movements from right to left. Eighth, she may raise her bust to show that she is reaching the height of her desire. Ninth, lying back again, she reveals that her pleasure is at its peak. And tenth, at the same time as she reaches her orgasm, her vagina releases a flow of liquid, containing her vital essence.

In any case, the balance between the partners ought to be perfect. A man and a woman must only make love if they are in complete harmony. Both of them must want it and go out to meet the other partner half-way. The sexual act can only be harmful for the two lovers if the woman desires the union and the man refuses it, or if the man is fired with passion without receiving any response from the woman. The *yin* and the *yang* must go out to meet each other. It is only thus that the two partners can obtain perfect happiness and a long life. The movements of the man and the woman must also correspond with their cosmic orientation.

This is how the sexual act will be performed: the two lovers will first of all take up a sitting position, the man on the left of the woman. Then the man will take the woman on to his knees, and after this they will lie down side by side in a slow progression. The woman will then fall back and will open her legs wide. The man will kneel down between her legs in a slow-motion movement. There will be caresses, sweet murmurs, embraces and kisses, with lips against lips and body against body, each of the couple gorging himself or herself on the saliva of the other. The man will nibble the lips or the tongue of his partner a little. Kisses and caresses, repeated a thousand times, will enable them to forget all the troubles and cares of this world. With her left hand the woman will take hold of the Jade Stem of her lover, while

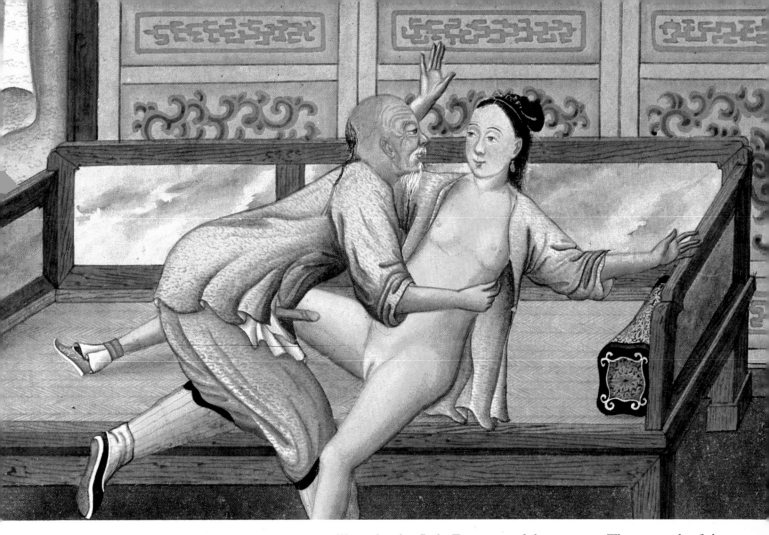

with his right hand the man will stroke the Jade Entrance of the woman. The strength of the *yin* that she will put forth will allow the Jade Stem to erect and to resemble, as it points straight up into the air, a steep lonely peak, a point in the Milky Way. The man's *yang*, on the other hand, will envelop the woman, provoking a heavy efflux of fluid, which will moisten the Vermilion Ravine, as a spring will fertilize the opening of a deep valley. The forces of the *yin* and the *yang* must be exerted in a spontaneous manner. Anything artificial in the methods used could lead to some internal disease for the man or for the woman. When the two partners have reached the threshold of happiness, they can enter in together, their thoughts at last liberated from all fear and all grief. One can unite with the other, and the Precious Doorway will open its lips to the Jade Stem, which will pass gently through a vast pine-forest before making its way into the depths of the cavern. Continuing with his kisses and his expression of passionate feelings, the man will allow his penis to play within this cave and will caress the stomach and the tips of the breasts of the woman. Thus both the man and the woman will be stirred up by desire, a feeling which will penetrate right to the very depths of their soul. The Vigorous Peak will rub against the Jade Veins as if in some light entertainment, preliminary to setting off on the road through the dark tunnel.

Liquid flows abundantly and swiftly down the Vermilion Ravine, while the Vigorous Peak pursues its penetration straight in. The two partners are no longer on earth and the man performs little rapid movements, thrusting and withdrawing his member. He takes it right out to wipe it, and when he puts it back in again, he gives little isolated thrusts, sometimes slow sometimes rapid, according to the rhythm of the twenty-one breaths. The woman, for her part, follows the movements of her partner. The Vigorous Peak inspects the whole of the back of the cavern with brief thrusts, sometimes with a rotating movement, according to the sexual parts of the feminine anatomy. Sou-nu has given a name to each part of the external sexual

"Concerning the questions of positions, the Tao does not recommend any as the one ideal position...
To make progress in the field of love and love-making, it is also necessary to experiment continually, and it is essential that each couple should find the position that suits them best as well as the most disturbing caresses and the sweetest kisses."

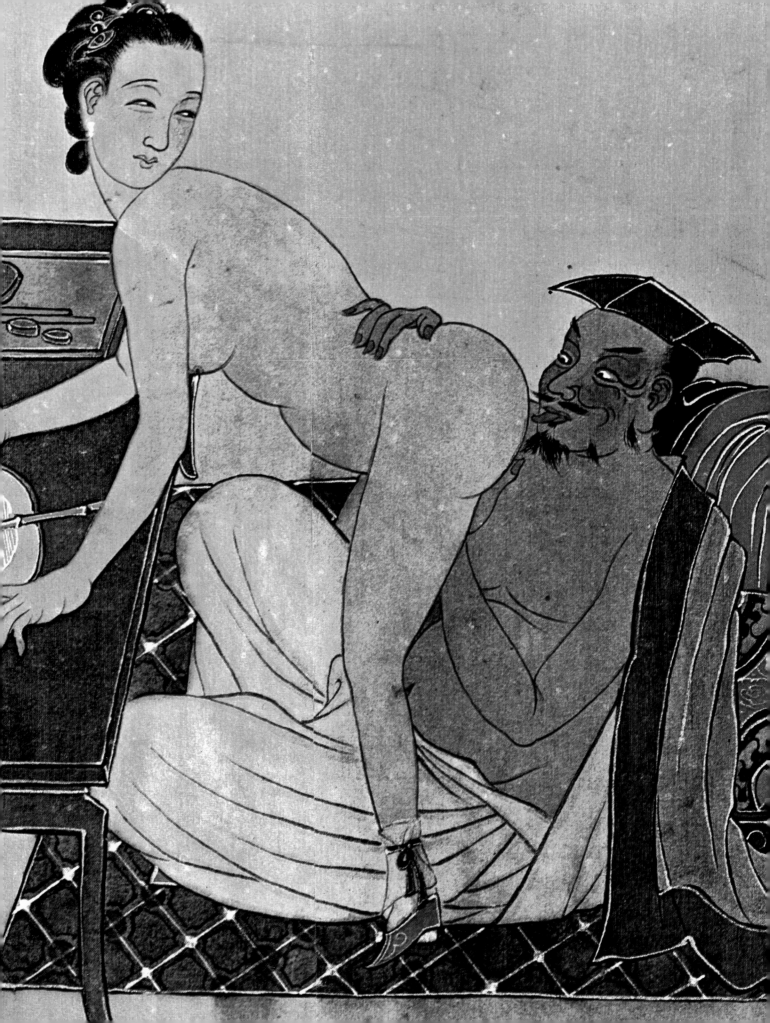

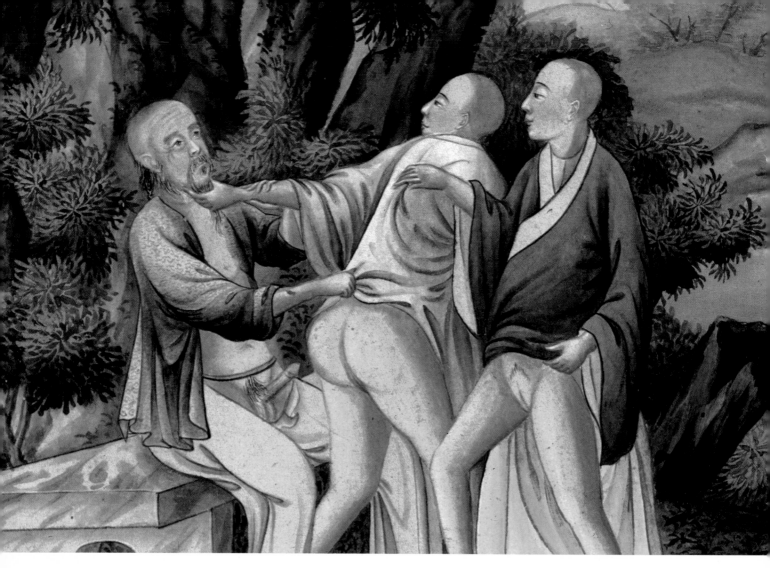

organs of the woman. Thus, two centimetres inside, one finds the Lute String, at twelve centimetre the Wheat Seed (the neck of the womb), the Jewel Terrace is none other than the clitoris; the Jade Veins refers to the place where the lips are joined below the vulva; the Golden Ravine is the upper part of the vulva...

According to the book of Tong-Hsuan, the Jade Stem can carry out nine different movements, and to explain this he makes use, on numerous occasions, of examples which he takes from the animal world. From left to right, and from right to left, it waves about exactly like a general cutting through the ranks of the enemy. Up and down, like a wild, rampaging horse jumping across a river. It goes in and out in just the same manner as seagulls playing above the waves. It gives short and long thrusts just like a sparrow pecking at grains of rice. Slight thrusts then deeper ones, performed in a regular manner, recall the stones that are worn away and rounded by the waves of the sea. It can creep forward slowly like a snake, which slides smoothly into a hole where it can spend the winter. It can wave about quickly, like a rat seized with panic, rise slowly, like a falcon holding a sheep in its claws, or can again move forward like a great sail, swelling with the gusts of a strong wind.

The same author gives us six ways of introducing the Jade Stem into a woman. Here they are: The Jade Stem should be pushed downwards and allowed to play on the Lute Strings, with a rhythmical sawing motion, shuttling to and fro. Then it should be thrust against the Bright Ravine above the Jade Veins, as if one were cutting away the outside of a hard fruit to reach the Jade core within. In and out the Jade Stem must go, entering and withdrawing. It must also move from right to left, like a blacksmith at his anvil soldering iron. Let the Vigorous Peak screw round and round within the Sacred Field and the Deep Valley,

18

"The fourth basic position, that in which the man takes the woman from behind, has five important variations."

like a farmer who digs and delves in his fields in autumn; and make the two peaks Hsuan-pou Peak and T'ien-T'ing Peak rub together. These are the two mythical summits which are crumbling away together.

METHODS

In the book *Hsuan-nu-king,* we learn from one of the replies given by the Girl with Jet-black Hair to the Yellow Emperor, that the Jade Stem should not be waved about in an attempt to help it to become erect. The member, on the contrary, must pass through four "states" in order to succeed in creating the eight "spirits" of the woman. Harmony is not to be expected, however, if one feels no movement stirring in the Jade Stem. The spirit of the skin is not yet aroused if it does not start swelling even slightly, the spirit of the bones remains numb and sluggish if it does not become hard, and if it does not give off any kind of heat at all, it is the heart which has remained asleep. A certain quivering shows that the semen is beginning to stir, and it builds up as the Stem gradually swells to become bigger and bigger. When the member hardens, the semen arrives near the inner door and it is the heat which will force it out. It is, therefore, necessary to have complete control over these four "spirits" if one is to perform the perfect sexual act.

The Emperor, eagerly seeking for advice, then asks what the nine "spirits" of the woman are that correspond to the man's four. And the Girl with Jet-black Hair answers him calmly and with a smile: "The spirit of the lungs is aroused in the woman when she begins to breath deeply and to swallow her saliva; the spirit of her heart when she murmurs sweet words of love and begins to give the man kisses; the spirit of her spleen when the takes her partner into her arms and hugs him close, and the spirit of her kidneys when her sexual organs become moist and slimy. When the woman sucks the tongue of her partner, that means that the spirit of her bones is awakening within her, while it is the spirit of the blood that drives her to take hold of the Jade Stem with her hands; and lastly it is the spirit of her flesh which makes her want to caress the man's nipples."

In the book *Yu-fang-pi-kine,* the beneficial effects of the sexual act are dealt with, and it is the Daughter of Candour who is given the task of describing these eight "therapeutic methods". During the first of them, the man stretches himself out between the woman's legs, and after having given her eighteen thrusts, he stops to allow a beneficial concentration of the semen. This will be performed twice a day over a period of fifteen days. This method is also intended to heal the wife's bleeding.

To obtain the second of the "benefits", the woman must lie on her back, with a cushion under her buttocks and with her legs stretched out. The man will then slide his penis into her, and interrupt his action after twenty-seven thrusts. This method can be used to bring rest to the mind and to cure vaginal disorders. It is to be prescribed three times a day over a period of twenty days.

A therapy for international organs consists of making the woman lie on her side, while the man places himself across her. The act is interrupted after thirty-six thrusts, but it must be performed four times a day, on twenty consecutive days.

One remedy that can be used to strengthen the bones is to perform the act in the following manner: the woman lies on her back, with her left knee bent. Her partner is stretched out on her and gives her forty-five thrusts; the purpose of this is to make his joints harmonize and to cure any congestion his companion may have.

To improve the circulation of the blood, the woman must lie on her right side and bend her right knee. The man enters her while supporting himself on his hands. He will not give more than forty-five thrusts. This method can be used for relieving any pains in the vagina.

To combat irregularities in the woman's menstruation and to give himself more strength, the man will lie on his back and will put his penis into the woman's body while she is in a crouching position, with her buttocks raised. The act should be performed in this way ten days running, with the man raising and lowering the body of this companion for the sixty-three thrusts he is to give her.

A remedy for treatment of the marrow is obtained by the following procedure: the man puts his penis into the woman from behind, the woman being in a lying position with her bottom raised. They will count up to seventy-two thrusts before stopping.

To harmonize and fortify the organism, the woman will be on her back, with her legs bent, and then man, with his legs spread wide, will give her eighty-one thrusts. This method will be used nine times a day over a period of nine days.

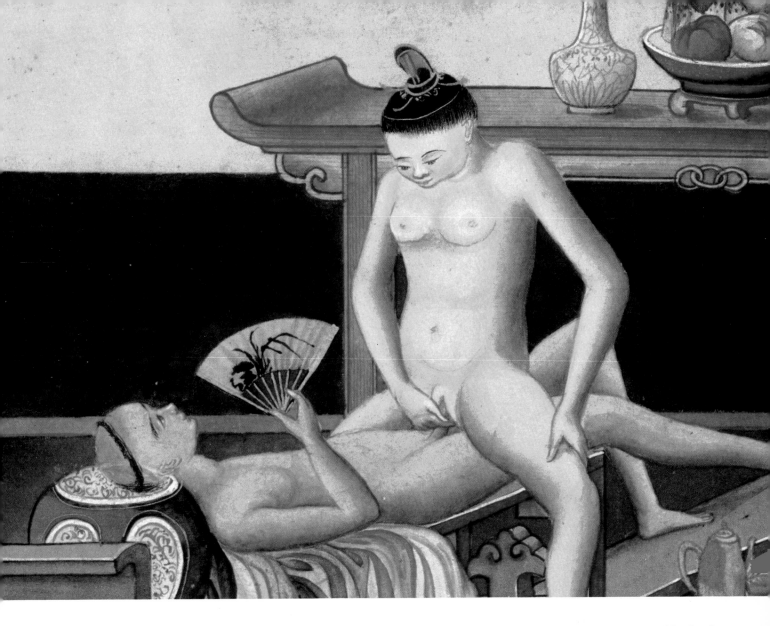

"According to the master Tong-hsuan, only thirty main positions exist. If one leaves aside the four classical positions there remain twenty-six others." Right; "Lying on his back, the man spreads his legs wide apart. The woman is sitting on him, her thighs well apart... Then the Vigorous Peak is pushed into the Precious Doorway."

CHARACTERISTICS OF IDEAL AND HARMFUL PARTNERS

In the manual *Yu-fang-pi-kine* it is stated that the man is well advised to choose for his love-making women who are young and rather plump, and it is also added that the women should, moreover, have breasts which are not yet completely formed, small eyes and hair as fine as silk. The ideal woman's bone structure should not be too big, and all the joints of her bones should be well covered with flesh. Her face must radiate sweetness and her speech must be as musical as possible. It is better if her pubis and armpits are not covered with hair, or if there is hair that it is soft and fine.

The Yellow Emperor then asks a few questions about the external signs which enable one to know if a woman is suitable for sexual intercourse or not. The Daughter of Candour enumerates for him the characteristics of the ideal woman. She must be tender and docile, with very fine black hair and smooth skin. The best female companions are of average size, that is, not too tall, nor too fat, nor too thin, nor too small. The woman's vagina will easily become moist, the lips and the vulva will be fairly thick and of a reasonable size. Her age will be somewhere between twenty-five and thirty, and she will not yet have had any children. It is recommended that the woman should have the temperament to move a great deal during the sexual act and that her vagina should discharge her liquid in abundance, to such an extent, even, that her partner will have difficulty in controlling it. Even if the man may not yet know the methods for the sexual act very well, he will choose his women in such a way that they will never do him any harm during intercourse.

The external signs which enable one to know that a woman is not fit to be chosen as a partner are very clear. They include different physical imperfections: a coarse complexion, a protuberant Adam's apple, irregular teeth or a wide mouth, eyes with a yellowish tinge or bloodshot, large prominent factor. Dishevelled hair is not acceptable, nor is downy hair on the upper lip, or on the cheeks. Yellowish hair is frowned upon, and long, stiff pubic hair is also a bad sign. The man risks losing his strength and ruining his health if he makes an approach to such women.

In the *T'ai-ts'ing-king*, it is recommended that, in order to be able to evaluate the qualities of a particular woman, one should carefully examine the hair of her pubis and of her armpits. The direction of the growth of the hair and whether or not it is curly, can indeed indicate that a woman has a cold body and hard bones, that she sometimes gives off an unpleasant odour, especially the odour of perspiration, and also that she has some heart disorder. It is clear that one should avoid copulating with a woman in whom one can recognize such signs.

On the other hand, hermaphrodites have the reputation of being very dangerous, as have women with a long clitoris, especially if it increases and decreases with the moon. This type of woman cannot bring a man any benefit.

One should also take into account the age of the partners, avoiding too great a difference in age. Copulation can be harmful for the woman if the man with whom she has intercourse is twice as old as she is, and harmful for the man if it is his partner who is older than he is. The partner, however, who practises the Tao represents no danger for the other partner, so that a man of sixty-five years old could give a young woman partner the benefit of his great control and his wide experience. In Ancient China, they did not have the same ideas about age as we have today, and a mature man could at that time be a perfect partner for love games. One even very frequently happened to hear the story of couples who were unhappy, although the man was young and handsome and his young partner seemed, at first sight, to have every reason to be satisfied with him. The example is also given of a great many happy couples, very much in love with each other and living in complete harmony, even if the man was no longer young and not at all good-looking. He knew, on the other hand, how to satisfy his wife. A difference in age between the partners was not considered to be abnormal or a sign of perversion.

They could see a certain number of advantages in the fact that there were such differences in age. Thus, when the man was more mature, he had his erection more slowly, and if the woman was young and had an abundance of fluid, he could introduce his penis easily into her her and, thanks to his knowledge of the Tao, reach a total erection gently and

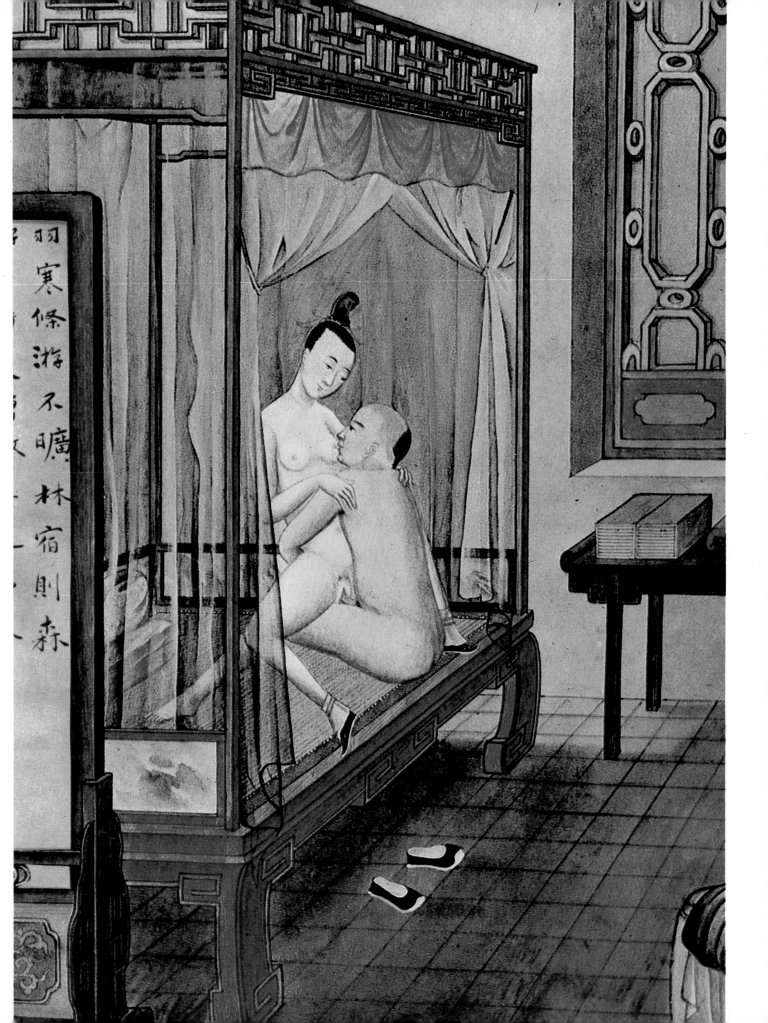

"When the woman places herself on top, the most usual way of performing the sexual act is to mount her partner, in the same way as if she were getting on a horse. But she can also, if she wishes, lie on him and kiss him on the mouth. She can carry out slow movements, with her chest and her abdomen, or make little shaking movements such as a fish makes when it finds itself cought in a net."

easily. Many women greatly appreciated this manner of doing things, gentler and pleasanter than the rapid erection of a young man, and his sudden penetration. Moreover, a young woman gives off a fresh odour which encourages the older man's excitement, and he in his turn provides a peaceful, confidential atmosphere to the act, which is not without its own charm. The man, also had a greater control over the relationship as a whole, which facilitated and increased the pleasure of the woman. The attraction was then reciprocal. The woman had, moreover, the advantage of experiencing with an older husband of a material security that she would never have had otherwise. It is for all these reasons that a great number of girls were very attracted by mature men, won over by their experience, their wisdom, their calmness, and their knowledge of the joys and of the worries of life. Their choice allowed them, moreover, to preserve an eternal youth, for they never had to be afraid that one day they would be abandoned for a woman companion whose charms were less tarnished.

The relationships between an older woman and a young man can also offer advantages for the two partners. A mature woman generally has, indeed, much more indulgence for the sexual difficulties of a very young man, difficulties that she takes into

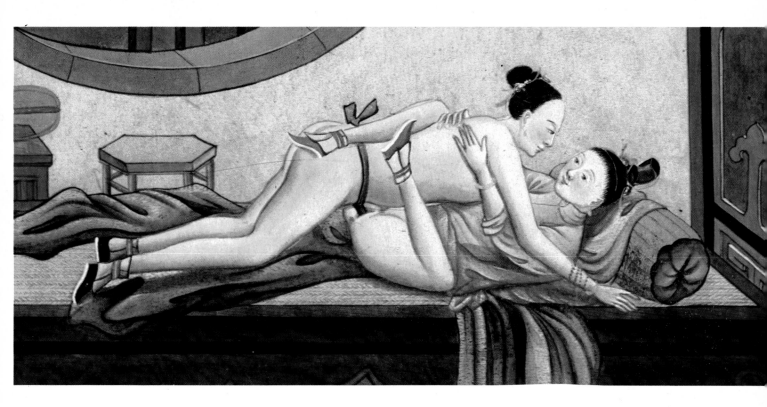

consideration although they would annoy her in a man of her own age. The youth of her partner will be for her a great source of "benefits" from a sexual point of view. In addition to this, her vagina having become wider with the years, the man will be able to control himself more easily; his penis, which will rise stiffly, will be able to stimulate his partner more. Indeed, certain young men prefer older women for the same reasons as those that make girls prefer more mature men. They find in their partner, if she is older than them, a perfect combination of maternal love and sexual love. Moreover, an orientation of the body according to the different seasons will render the sexual intercourse even more beneficial. Thus, one will lie with one's head towards the east in the spring, with one's head towards the south in the summer, towards the west in the autumn and to the north in the winter.

During the month, the odd dates are favourable for love-making, whereas the even dates are unfavourable.

The most suitable period of the day for copulation is from one o'clock in the morning until noon, and the least suitable from noon to eleven o'clock at night.

In the *Yi-king,* in the Book of Changes, one is advised, in order to see that one's sexual life runs smoothly, as well as one's way of life in other respects, to learn how to differentiate between what is suitable and what is harmful, by means of signs which are sent to us by Heaven. Man must feel a sort of respect mingled with a touch of terror when "above his head" appear signs of something unusual, or when disasters present themselves "at his feet". He will not take these warnings lightly and will take care not to upset the cosmic forces. To organize his sexual life, man will pay careful attention to the influence of the *yin* and the *yang* in the cosmos.

Thus he will not copulate at times of great heat or in very cold weather, when the wind is wild, or when the rain is falling in torrents, nor during an earthquake or a heavy storm, nor while an eclipse of the sun or of the moon is taking place. For these are the taboos of Heaven. He will also take into account, though, man's taboos, and abstain from having sexual relations after a heavy meal or under the effects of drink. He will also abstain, without exception, at times when he has been experiencing great fear, when he is feeling depressed, worried or considerably agitated.

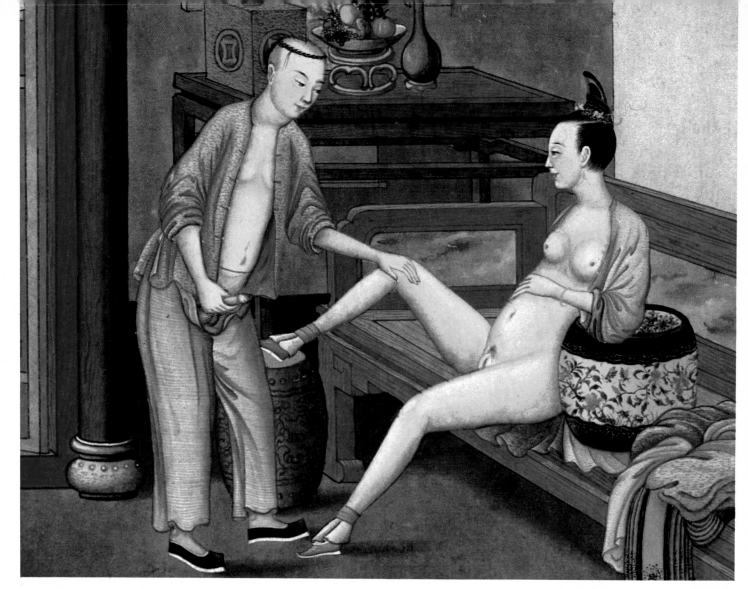

"During the month, the odd dates are favorable for love-making. The most suitable period of the day for copulation is from one o'clock in the morning until noon." Right: "The man and the woman remain standing, face to face. Entwined, they kiss each other in turn."

Never will a man and a woman copulate near temples or places of worship, in places where the spirits of Heaven and of Earth are venerated, nor anywhere near a fire or a well.

Methods or instruments intended to increase the enjoyment of sexual union by artificial means are not to be used. Certain women, for example, drive into their vagina an ivory penis or a small bag filled with flour, in order to satisfy their desires; they are only "thieves of life" and old age will be their lot earlier than for their contemporaries. And the Daughter of Candour adds that one should not partake of the sexual act on the day when Heaven and Earth are coupling, this day being the sixteenth day of the fifth moon. Those who do so, will die before three years have passed.

After a very serious illness, the man and the woman will abstain from sexual relations for a hundred days in order to give their vital essence sufficient time to recover its strength. The Daughter of Candour quotes, by way of warning, the example of a nobleman who, only eight days after recovering from a very high temperature, thought that he was completely cured the moment he could walk normally and ride a horse. He decided, then, to make love with one of his women friends, which produced in him violent convulsions and very sharp and strong abdominal pains. He died the very next day.

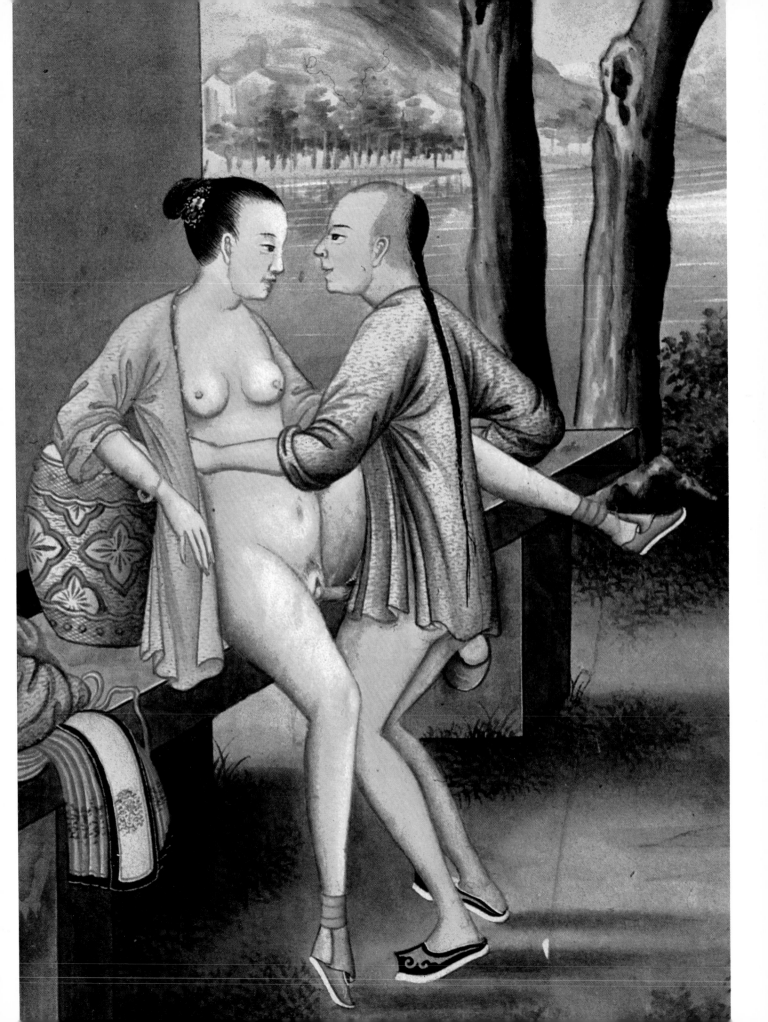

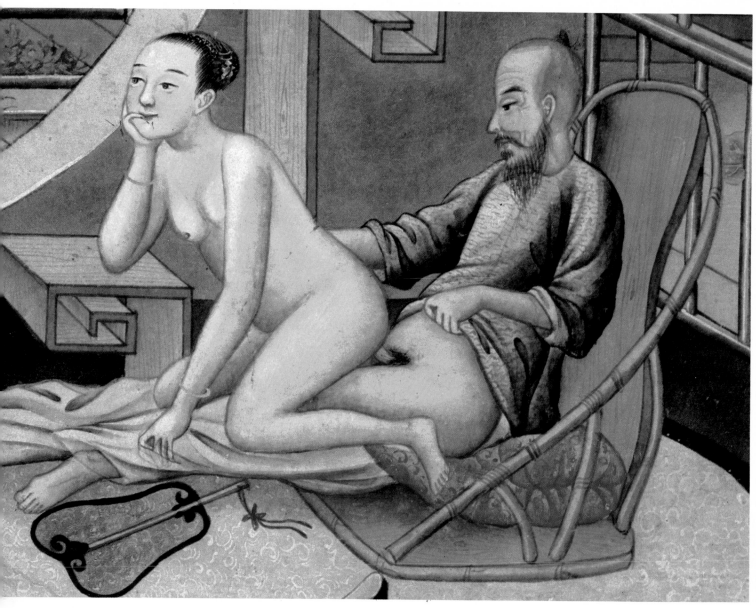

"The movements of introduction and withdrawal will be carried out very slowly... The man will avoid the emission of his semen. If he manages to copulate a number of times during one single night, and to avoid ejaculating, the duration of his live will be prolonged."

It is, of course, necessary too to abstain completely from sexual intercourse with demons and witches. If a person allows himself to be carried away and falls into debauchery, his desires will become stronger and stronger each time. Nightmare figures will take advantage of the situation and will copulate with the person in question in the form of a human. Their art is very subtle and the victim will fall into their power before dying a lingering death, even in the midst of delightful pleasures.

To have proof of the existence of these nightmare figures, Pong-tsuo recommends that one should go alone into some particularly marshy spot, lost up in the mountains. There one should stop, and look about vaguely in space, thinking with all one's concentration of pleasant erotic games. Gradually, the view will become blurred and the body will change temperature constantly, going from hot to cold and then becoming hot again. At the end of three whole days, a nightmare figure of the opposite sex will appear before the waiting person, who will welcome him or her, and the pleasure produced by this meeting will be three times

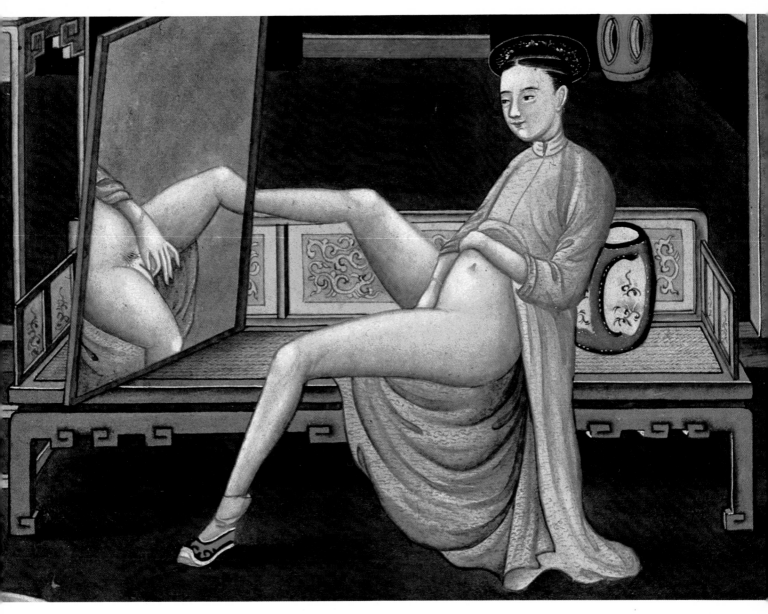

as great as the pleasure experienced with the best possible human partner. At the same time, however, a terrible, insidious disease will have penetrated into the body of the unknowing adventurer.

POSITIONS AND SELF-KNOWLEDGE

Concerning the questions of positions, the Tao does not recommend any as the one ideal position, since this will depend on the temperament of the different couples. Amongst them, there will not be two whose physical shape, weight and size of body and sexual organs correspond with each other... not to mention the differences in behaviour linked with passion, timidity, tenderness and the joy of being in each other's company. As a general rule, all the manuals give the four classical positions, as well as a certain number of variations, but they present them rather as suggestions than anything else. The teaching of the Tao is that one must progress in all these fields, and that knowledge of oneself is of prime importance if one wants to attain perfection. It is for this reason that there is a warning in the Tao against establishing a routine in one's sexual life. To make progress in the field of love and love-

"When the two partners have reached the threshold of happiness, they can enter in together. One can unite with the other, and the Precious Doorway will open its lips to the Jade Stem, which will pass gently through a vast pine-forest before making its way into the depths of the cavern... Both the man and the woman will be stirred up by desire, a feeling which will penetrate right to the very depths of their soul."

making, it is also necessary to experiment continually, and it is essential that each couple should find the position that suits them best as well as the most disturbing caresses and the sweetest kisses.

To achieve this, it is not a question of copying what the manuals say. They are nothing but a simple guide, giving information from which one can start one's own investigation. The Ancient Chinese, always eager to go further and further into the problems of self-knowledge, with this in mind, made use of the "benefits" of perfectly performed love-making.

The four basic positions are the following : the man places himself above the woman; the woman takes the upper position and the man the lower position; the man and the woman both lie on their side, sometimes one on the right side and sometimes the other; the man introduces his penis into the vagina of the woman from behind.

Starting from these four positions, there can be any number of variations if one takes into account the difference in size between the partners, the situation of the vagina of the woman etc. There can also sometimes be a change of position in the course of the same sexual act. Let us take as an example the position where the woman is first lying on the side face to face with her partner, and then finds herself, as the result of a rolling movement of the two bodies, lying on top of him. This change of position is easy to carry out in a big bed or on a blanket placed on the ground. More athletic couples manage to perform it even in a very confined space. There are two main advantages which result from this manœuvre : when the woman is a little shy, or inexperienced this rolling movement succeeds in placing her above her partner in a completely natural way, almost without her being conscious of it; this will help her to begin to take a more active part in the act of intercourse, which will thus better satisfy her erotic needs. For a great many women who are a little frigid, or slightly hesitant when faced with the sexual act, this position will give her a much better chance of reaching an orgasm.

The second advantage of this change of position is felt by the man, especially if he is already getting old, or his energy is not as resistant as it was, and he finds himself face to face with a woman younger than he is and full of vigour. In this case it is the woman, in fact, who makes the greater effort, while the man, completely relaxed, achieves the greater pleasure. By using the effect of this rolling movement, the man has no need to withdraw his member in order to bring about this change in their positions, which is most beneficial to those whose erection falters the very moment that they withdraw their member from the vagina of the woman.

When the woman places herself on top, the most usual way of performing the sexual act is to mount her partner, in the same way as if she were getting on a horse. But she can also, if she wishes, lie on him and kiss him on the mouth, all the time keeping her legs well open, or even sometimes closed firmly one against the other. She can carry out slow movements, from the right and from the left, with her chest and her abdomen, which are clinging closely to the body of the man, or she can make little shaking movements such as a fish makes when it finds itself caught in a net, which can produce a very keen pleasure in a great many women. An expert woman can manage, while sitting on a man as if she were on a horse, to turn in a complete circle and to find herself facing towards the feet of her partner.

30

The fourth basic position, that in which the man takes the woman from behind, has five important variations : the man and the woman are lying on the bed one beside the other; the man is stretched out on the back of his companion, and she raises her buttocks; the woman kneels on the bed and the man remains standing on the floor; the man is seated and the woman sits on him and finally, the woman can lean against a tree or a wall, with her body in a sloping position, and the man penetrates her from a standing position.

As far as the other positions are concerned, we shall follow for these the indications of the master Tong-hsuan, for whom there only exist thirty main positions. If one leaves aside the four classical positions, which we have just described above, there remain twenty-six others, which are as follows:

The Ball of Wool. The woman, lying on her back, firmly clasps the man's neck in her arms, and twines her legs around the middle of his body. The man leans on the back of the woman's thighs, embraces her and slips the Jade Stem into her.

The Dragon Figure. The woman, lying on her back, bends her legs and raises them high. The man, on his knees between her open thighs, pushes the woman's feet backwards with his left hand and, drawing them up above his chest, he at the same time and with his right hand thrusts the Jade Stem into the Precious Doorway.

The Fish Kiss. The man and the woman are here both in a lying position, their bodies as if they had been welded together, thigh to thigh, face to face. The woman puts one of her legs on the man's leg. As they kiss each other, they suck each other's tongue. Then the man, with his legs wide apart, lifts the raised leg of the woman higher with his hand, and thrusts the Jade Stem into his partner.

The Migratory Birds. The woman lying on her back opens her legs wide. The man, sitting on her with his legs apart, leans forward and clasps her neck in his arms. The woman, being entwined more closely around the middle of her body, allows the Jade Stem to enter deep into the Vermilion Ravine.

Frantic Flight. The woman, lying on her back, takes hold of one of her feet with each hand. Meanwhile the man kneels down with his legs spreadeagled, and twines himself around the middle of the woman's body. Then he thrusts the Jade Stem in as far as the Lyre Strings.

The Mandarin's Figure. The woman, who is lying on her side, curves both her legs and places the left one on the man's right thigh. Then the man, who is lying behind her, places his left leg on the calf of the woman's right leg. Raising the woman's thigh with his left knee, he

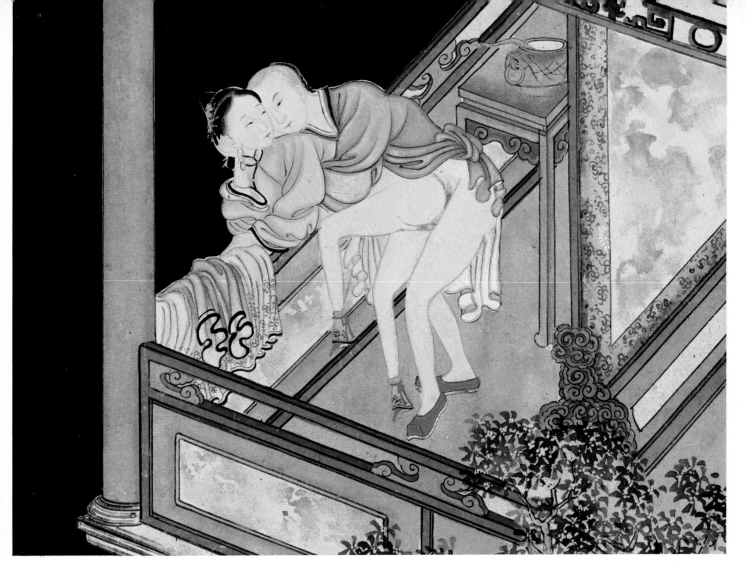

"Even if the man may not yet know the methods for the sexual act very well, he will choose his women in such a way that they will never do him any harm during intercourse."

thrusts the Jade Stem into her.

As Lively as Butterflies. Lying on his back, the man spreads his legs wide apart. The woman is sitting on him, her thighs well apart, her face turned in his direction, her feet placed on the bed. She writhes strongly about, as she supports herself on her hands, and then the Vigorous Peak is pushed into the Precious Doorway.

The Flight of the Upside-Down Swan. The man lies on his back and then opens his legs wide. The woman sits down on his abdomen, her legs spreadeagled, her face turning towards the man's feet. Lowering her head, she takes hold of the Jade Stem, and slides it into the Vermilion Ravine.

The Tree Figure. The woman, lying on her back, raises her arms and folds them across her chest. The man takes her into his arms, holding her around the middle, while the woman twines her arms around the middle of the man's body. Thus it is that the Jade Stem is thrust into the Precious Doorway.

Stiff as Bamboo Canes. The man and the woman remain standing, face to face. Entwined, they kiss each other in turn. The Vigorous Peak weighs so heavily on the Vermilion Ravine that it finishes by making its entrance on to the Yang Terrace.

The Dance of the Golden Hens. The man tells one woman to lie down on her back; and he tells the other to sit down on her. The woman lying underneath raises her arms, while the

"Even if the retention of the semen is a very simple act, few people manage to achieve it... This "reversal of the semen" is a point that is insisted on in Taoism. It is, in fact, written that a man must in no circumstances think of satisfying his desire in the course of the sexual act, (but) must control it completely in order to manage to nourish his vital essence."

other one is sitting on her, with her thighs apart, in such a way that the vulva of the one is almost touching the vulva of the other. The man kneels down, turning to face them; he can thus make his way into the Jade Entrances, first the top one, then the lower one.

The Cock and its Chick. This way of copulating is a most suitable method when a tall and stout woman is making love, with a short man as her partner.

Gliding Flight. The man, standing up in front of the bed, raises the woman's legs up high. Then he thrusts the Jade Stem as deeply as possible into the Precious Doorway.

A Ride in Natural Surroundings. The woman is lying flat on her back. Then the man lifts up her legs and places them on his shoulders. When he has done this, he thrusts the Jade Stem deep into the Precious Doorway.

A Frenzied Gallop. The woman is lying on the bed, flat on her back. The man lowers himself gently and with his left hand draws her head towards him, while with his right hand, he raises her feet. Then he thrusts the Jade Stem as far as possible into the Precious Gateway.

Like a Mad Foal. The woman is lying flat on the bed on her back. The man places one of her feet on his own shoulder, while the other moves about freely. The reason for this posture is that it allows the Jade Stem to penetrate right into the depths of the Vermilion Ravine, and with the most exquisite sexual pleasure.

The Bound of a Wild Beast. The woman, leaning her weight on her hands and her knees, lowers her head forwards; meanwhile the man kneels behind her, entwining her in his embrace around the middle of her body. He then thrusts the Jade Stem in through the Doorway.

The Insect Against the Trunk Figure. The woman, lying on the bed on her stomach, opens wide her legs. The man, lowering himself carefully between the woman's thighs, lifts her legs up. Embracing her, he thrusts the Jade Stem into the Precious Doorway from behind.

Stuck against the Tree. The man sits down on the bed, his legs crossed. To the woman, who has her back towards him, he says that she must sit on his lap. She then lowers her head and watches attentively the way in which the Jade Stem is introduced into her. Then the man quickly embraces her around the middle of her body, and starts to move with a rocking motion.

Sweet Birds in the Breeze. The man sits down on the bed, with his legs crossed. He tells a girl to sit down in his lap, with her face turned in his direction, and he then thrusts the Jade Stem deep into the precious Doorway. Another woman, who is behind the girl, helps the girl with her movements by shaking the tail of the little coat the girl is wearing. This is certainly a good way of bringing forth the height of pleasure.

Games in a Cavern. The woman, lying on her back, raises her legs high in the air, while holding her feet. The man, having placed himself facing her, kneels down and introduces the Jade Stem into the Vermilion Ravine. Then he starts to move back and forth, with his hands supporting him on the bed. This posture quickly creates a voluptuous effect.

Flight above Infinity. The woman stretches herself out on the bed, lying on her back, and the man then places her leg against the top of his arms. Down below, with his arms under the

woman's body, around her waist, he introduces the Jade Stem into her.

The Groaning Tree Kiss. The man, sitting crosslegged, tells the woman to crouch in his lap, and winds his arms around her. He puts one hand under her buttocks, and with the other hand he slips the Jade Stem into the woman. Then, leaning on the bed with that hand, he begins to move backwards and forwards.

United like a Cat and Mouse. The man is lying on his back with his legs wide apart. The woman places herself opposite him, and lying down on him, introduces the Jade Stem into her vagina. Or the man lies on the woman's back and with his Jade Stem plays around inside the Precious Doorway.

Copulation at the End of Springtime. The woman crouches on the bed, leaning on his hands and his knees. The man, standing beside the bed, embraces her with his arms around her waist, and thrusts the Jade Stem into the Precious Doorway. Without any doubt, this method leads rapidly to the heights of sexual pleasure.

Race at the Beginning of Autumn. The woman crouches on her hands and knees. The man, leaning the upper part of his body over the woman's back, lowers his head and thrusts the Jade Stem into the Jade Entrance."

THE RETENTION OF THE SEMEN

A considerable part of sexual manuals based on Taoism is devoted to the control of ejaculation. In one of these works it is said that the most consummate Art in sexual relationships consists in copulating with ten women in a single night, without ejaculating even one single time. The great secret of life is, indeed, to have intercourse without discharging any semen. This semen will return into the body and will give the organism back all its vitality.

"*It is better not to take undue advantage of the presence of very beautiful women, for they will bring one too easily to the point of ejaculation, and too great a flow of semen tires the veins and blood-vessels.*"

For the Taoists, sexual intercourse is intended to prolong life and to bring about in the two partners the vital current which starts in the head and reaches right down to the sexual organs by means of the spine. At the moment when the semen is held back, the vital impulse shoots away from the sexual organs to reach first the kidneys, after making a detour through the navel, before continuing upwards through the vertebrae, from where it eventually arrives at the heart. The current then continues its journey as far as Ni-hoan, which is situated above the brain and zenith of vitality. It is then that a sun and a moon begin to shine around the head, and that the masculine and feminine principles make man immortal.

Even if the retention of the semen is a very simple act, or so we are told in the *Yu-fang-tche-yao*, few people manage to achieve it. And this is a great pity, since the fact of performing coition a large number of times in one day without ejaculating can cure all ills, all diseases.

This "reversal of the semen" is a point that is insisted on in Taoism, and is peculiar to it. It is, in fact, written that a man must in no circumstances think of satisfying his desire in the course of the sexual act. Not at all. He must control it completely in order to manage to nourish his vital essence. He will never give free rein to his passion, nor force his body into extravagance in this domain; he will, on the other hand, think of the beneficial effects which will result from the sexual act, and of his health, which he will preserve thanks to it, even at any advanced age that he may reach.

That is why he will be moderate in following his impulses during the period of his youth, and will show himself to be very sparing in the distribution of his semen.

But the Yellow Emperor continues to seek answers to his questions. For him, real

"The man lies on his back and then opens his legs wide. The woman sits down on his abdomen, her legs spreadeagled, her face turning towards the man's feet..." The name of this position is "The Flight of the Upside-Down Swan".

pleasure consists, precisely, in ejaculating during the sexual act. If he has to restrain himself, how will he be able to get any pleasure from it?

The reply is not long in coming: each time that the man discharges his semen, his body is filled with an intense feeling of tiredness, sleep closes his eyes, he is thirsty, his limbs suffer from inertion, as if they were dead, and he hears a distant buzzing in his ears. In spite of what one might think, these are not the signs of true sexual satisfaction, even if they follow on after a moment of ectasy. On the other hand, each time that he performs the sexual act without ejaculating, his vital essence becomes stronger, his sight and his hearing take on a perfect clearness. He has perhaps repressed his passion, but his love itself remains intact. Is that not the very height of voluptuousness, to know that one will never possess enough the woman that one desires?

The Yellow Emperor replies that he would like to know with more precision what the benefits of the sexual act without any discharge of semen really are, and the Daughter of Candour, always ready to give any explanations she can, adds the following: If the man performs the sexual act once without ejaculating, his vital essence increases in vigour. If he succeeds in reversing the semen towards his internal regions twice, his senses of hearing and sight will develop to attain a maximum of intensity. If he manages to copulate three times in this way, his diseases will be cured. After four sexual acts without ejaculation, his soul will find complete serenity and after the fifth, the circulation of his blood will benefit from a great improvement. After the sixth time, his kidneys will become considerably stronger, and the seventh will see his buttocks and his thighs gain in strength and in force. After the eighth act, his whole body will be bursting with health. After the ninth, he will be sure to have a long life before him, and the tenth will put him on the road to immortality.

In another passage, the Yellow Emperor asks the Daughter of Candour how it is possible ever to have a child if one is for ever practising this method of economizing semen, and if the reversal of the semen to its source is the correct way to copulate. Everything depends on the physical condition and on the age of the individual, replied the Daughter of Candour. One must reach the point of being able to normalize one's ejaculations according to one's vital essence. One must never put pressure on one's mind or on one's body during sexual intercourse. Every time that one allows the semen to flow freely, the organism will suffer. A young man at the height of his form can allow himself to reach an orgasm twice a day; but if he is not in such good condition, even if he is only twenty years old, he will have to content himself with copulating once every twenty-four hours. At the age of thirty, strong, vigorous men can discharge semen once a day, and those in a less fit physical condition, once every two days.

At forty years old, a man in good health must realize that, even if he is still vigorous, he is going to begin gradually to lose his strength. He will wait until certain illnesses have found their way into his system and then will take a number of precautions. This is an age that marks a turning point in the life of a man, and it will become more important than ever for him to know in detail and in depth all there is to know about the Art of the Bedroom. He will only allow himself to reach an orgasm every three days, or at most every four days, according to his vigour. At the age of fifty, he must let at least five days pass between two orgasms, and men of a weaker constitution should even allow an interval of about ten days. At sixty years old, the strongest men will ejaculate every ten days, whereas the others will have to be content with one orgasm every twenty days. And at seventy, a strong man will

limit himself to a discharge of semen every thirty days, while those who are in less vigorous condition will abstain completely.

Account must also be taken of the periods in life when desire is more intensely felt. There are, indeed, men who, because of their increased virility, cannot remain for a very long time without ejaculating. This might produce in them on eruption of boils or other infections. After about the age of sixty, however, if a man avoids any opportunity for having his excitement aroused for a period of a month or two, he will then be able to abstain also from all sexual intercourse.

Again, the Daughter of Candour illustrates the soundness of her remarks by means of an example. A farmer came to see her and told her that his *yang* essence had been so powerful for a week that he felt a strong desire to copulate all the time in order to reach an orgasm.

She replied that such a desire could bring about some misfortune, since he made her think of an oil-lamp, which at first burns very gently, then just before it goes out, bursts into a final bright flame. "You are too old to permit yourself the luxury of such outbursts of activity. Abstain rather from copulating, and look after yourself well!" But the man did not take her advice seriously and continued to take his pleasure in the sexual act... but not for long. A week later, he was in his grave.

Every man who knows how to preserve his vitality makes sparing use of his generous sexual urges. If he does not control his passion, it is as if he were taking a little of the oil out of a lamp whose contents are already almost exhausted. When he retains his semen, on the other hand, it is as if he were adding oil to his lamp.

Lieo King adds that one can release one's semen once every three days in the spring, but only twice a month in the summer and autumn. In winter, on the other hand, one ought to abstain from ejaculating. It is only in taking into account these limits that a man can achieve longevity. An ejaculation in winter means a loss of *yang* energy three times as great as in the spring.

The man who has the good fortune to have concubines can perform the sexual act with them, making the semen flow back again and preventing ejaculation. In this way, he will absorb, by means of his penis, the secretions of the woman's vagina, at the same time as he

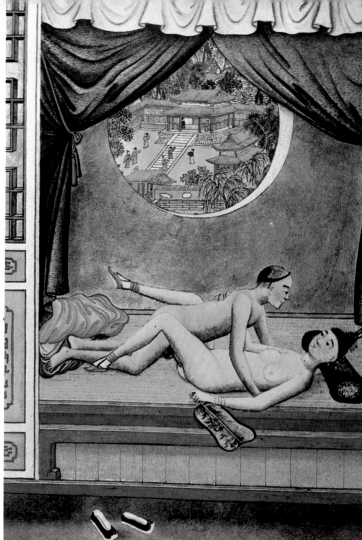

"One can count ten sorts of movements of the woman's body during the sexual act." — "It was considered to be essential that the woman should reach an orgasm during each union."

swallows his saliva, and his virility will thus be reinforced. Thus, when he has sexual intercourse with his wife, he will be sure that the children which may possibly be born from their union will be in good health.

As semen is a very precious substance, it is necessary to compensate for its loss after coition by taking possession of the woman's essence. To achieve this, one has to give nine thrusts of no great depth, followed by one deep thrust. And so that the semen returns by the same route as it has come by, and can protect life and do good to the organism, it is necessary to exert slight pressure below the member with the fingers, and only with the fingers of the left hand. The penis must play out its little games in the space situated between the Lute Strings and the Cavern in the shape of a Seed. The man will concentrate with all his attention, with his eyes tightly shut, will place his tongue against his palate, and will stretch his neck to its full length, arching his back at the same time. He will flare his nostrils, so that they are wide open, closing his mouth and breathing deeply. He will thus be able to retain his ejaculation, and the semen will flow back in the direction of the top of his head. Out of ten acts of intercourse, the man will content himself with ejaculating only two or three times.

In the *Treatise of Immortality* the great Lu explains in detail the method for the retention of semen, but asks his disciples to swear to keep the secret, and to seal their oath with their blood. Some inexperienced people might, indeed, not be able to apply this method correctly and this would result in serious physical complications for them. He says that, when a man feels an orgasm coming on, he must firmly press a point situated between the anus and the

"Some people still believe today in the idea that the Chinese have never been accustomed to kissing. It is true that they were not used to kissing in public, but the erotic, passionate kiss on the lips and the mouth were even considered to be an indispensable part of sexual intercourse."

testicles, with the first and the middle fingers of the left hand, breathing deeply, and grinding his teeth several times, but without holding his breath. The semen will then return back along the Jade Stem, and it is thus that he will succeed in living for a long time.

The Expert advises people who have a great deal of experience in the field of medicine or acupuncture, to play with the woman's body and to drink in her saliva or her Jade Fluid. It is in this manner that the desire will become more intense between the man and the woman. Moreover, the man will leave his penis very deeply implanted in the woman's vagina. He will take a rest in this position, before taking possession of the woman's secretions. When he is on the point of ejaculation and when he feels that the semen is on the move, the man will exert pressure with the fingers of his left hand on the *P'ing-yi* point or else, if he has enough time, pierce it with a thin needle. This point is situated about two centimetres above the right nipple, and with the *Three Yang* point, which is situated twelve centimetres above the heel, enables the sexual impulses to be effectively controlled. The man must imagine that his essence is brilliant red in colour, and is situated first of all in the lower part of the abdomen, and that it is divided into a sun and a moon in movement. Thanks to this swinging movement, it will rise gradually towards the place called *Ni-hoan*, situated inside the head, level with the eyes. It is there that the sun and the moon, which are about five centimetres in diameter, will finish by dissolving. The man will straighten his spine, will breathe in deeply, hold his breath, compress the bottom part of his body and then, breathing freely now, will withdraw his member. In this way, the semen will flow back to carry its benefits even as far as the brain.

Copulation on horseback is sought by those who succeed. The noble animal sometimes gives the rhythm...

THREE SORTS OF KISSES

Some people still believe today in the idea that the Chinese have never been accustomed to kissing. It is true that they were not used to kissing in public, as many western peoples do when they greet each other. Certain specialists even claim that instead of greeting each other with a kiss, they rubbed their noses together and gave a traditional little sniff. This idea perhaps comes from the custom that the Chinese had of inhaling the odour of little children from close up and in public, breathing in the special sweet perfume that all very small children give off, in order to greet them and to have themselves the pleasure of inhaling this sweet freshness and tenderness of childhood.

But kissing certainly took place in the intimacy of private life. The erotic, passionate kiss on the lips and the mouth were even considered to be an indispensable part of sexual intercourse, precisely because it allowed an exchange of vital essence, which is one of the ways of harmonizing the *yin* and the *yang*.

According to Taoists, there exist three distinctly different sorts of kiss.

The first was called the kiss of the Red Lotus. The man puts his tongue into the two cavities which are to be found under the woman's tongue. This is very beneficial for the male partner, who will gently suck these two little holes. The second type of kiss is given the name of the Twin Hills. This kiss is given to the very tips of the breasts and is very sweet to taste. This is most beneficial, not only to the man but also to the woman, since it is good for the circulation of her blood, soothes her body and her soul, and gives her a feeling of well-being. It also encourages the secretion of liquid, in both her mouth and her vulva.

The third kiss is the one called "of the Cave of the White Tiger" or sometimes also "Of

The horse seems to participate in certain poses and exercises; unless it only thinks of sniffing the ground, waiting for the meeting on his back to finish.

the Dark Door". This kiss is given on the external sexual organs of the woman. The Palace of the *Yin* opens slowly and the great pleasure experienced by the woman is revealed by the colour of her face, and by the murmurs that she utters. In addition, it is extremely good for the two partners.

For Taoism, the erotic kiss was considered to be of the highest importance in the Art of Love. The kiss bestowed on the private parts of both the man and the woman were thought to be a way of rousing all the senses of one's partner, even the most deeply hidden and the most sluggish. Kisses were for the Ancient Chinese, experts in the Art of Love, as important as they were simple. They were given in all naturalness, and on any part of the body of both the man and the woman, and they made use not only of the lips and the tongue, but also, on occasion, the teeth as well. Passionate kisses could sometimes be more revealing than an act of coition carried out as if it were part of a routine. The lips and the tongue evoked the idea of the vulva and the phallus, of which they possessed some of the characteristics, the only difference being that one can kiss for longer, since it is much easier to control the muscles of the lips and tongue than those of the sexual parts, and continue the kiss even after one has reached the height of the most absolute sexual pleasure.

Let it be remembered especially that perfect harmony is indispensable if the kisses are to be not only enjoyable but also passionate. The contact that joins the tongues and the lips of the two partners must be happy and relaxed if the pleasure is to be keen, and if the vital essence is to be enriched. Indeed, if the mouth remains tight and tense, how can the rest of the body possible become relaxed and be receptive to the caresses offered? The more the mouth opens to receive the pleasure that is available, the more easily the rest of the body will follow suit. Kissing demands the setting in motion and the participation of all the senses: touch,

*"The man will not copulate at times
of great heat or in very cold weather,
when the wind is wild, or when the
rain is falling in torrents... nor while
an eclipse of the sun or of the moon
is taking place."*

smell, taste and even hearing and sight. It is for this reason that Taoism again always recommends a high level of hygiene for the whole of the body. It also demands that great care be taken of general health, and that one abstain from eating and drinking anything with a very strong taste or smell, unless the partner has eaten or drunk the same thing at the same time. For any exception to this rule might produce in the other partner a sort of contraction or feeling of disgust, which might provoke a separation between the *yin* and the *yang*... A relationship which is not harmonious could, of course, certainly not be in the least beneficial.

EROTIC LITERATURE

In the T'ang period, as well as manuals on sex of an especially didactic nature, and intended to enlighten married couples, other works were produced to meet the demands of a public which was interested in a literature which was more or less erotic. All kinds of novels and short stories thus saw the light of day and were very successful. These manuscripts were passed from hand to hand, but they disappeared almost completely in the course of the following centuries, destroyed by the use that was made of them, or falling prey to the censors. Some of them, very mutilated, have however come down to us, and have taken their place in private collections. One of them, *the Poetic Song on Perfect Joys,* owed its preservation simply to the fact that it had been copied by order of a viceroy of China, Toan Fang, during the first decade of the present century. On the first page, the author announces that, if the reader finds certain passages obscene he must not be offended, for these descriptions are important to explain the joy of sexual union, "which is the greatest and the most complete of all the joys that the world possesses". The book describes all the moments in the life of a man, from his birth to his death, in a light, poetic tone, which aims rather at amusing the reader than at instructing him. It goes without saying that the author insists especially on subjects which are linked with erotism. Concerning the sexual act, he describes a couple who, quietly, one moonlit night at the beginning of spring, are standing alone beside a window, breathing in all the different odours of the night. The two partners read together the explanations of the Daughter of Candour and look carefully at the illustrations showing the different postures. They remain in silence for a moment, then the man begins to open the woman's embroidered trousers slowly. Her legs and her buttocks are the colour of jade. The woman then unfastens the man's trousers and takes hold of his Jade Stem. The two begin to become excited and exchange kisses. When the woman has finished undressing herself completely, and the man has too, they look at each other, examining their partner from head to foot. Their minds become confused and their eyes are veiled with a sort of mist. He caresses her slowly and gently from the head right down to the feet; they kiss each other on the mouth and suck each other's tongue. She offers the man her vulva, so that he can moisten it with his saliva and caress it. Then she raises her legs and places them on her partner's shoulders. The Jade Stem, with little trembling movements, raises its head aloft in an imperious manner, and the Golden Hole half opens its lips. The membrum virile is a solitary peak directed towards the heavens,

50

"There can also sometimes be a change of position in the course of the same sexual act."

and the Deep Cavern is a dark valley, moist and welcoming. The woman lies back on cushions, full of joy and pleasure, while the man supports himself on his hands and draws near with his penis. It advances and then withdraws again, and plays about, moving from right to left and back again, before making a quick, well-aimed thrust, which will take it to the level of the Lyre Strings. The man attacks, draws himself back, and goes from top to bottom, as if he wished to find the furthest depths in which to hide himself. The two partners move their buttocks one after the other, as in a joyful and passionate dance. The penis gives alternate short and deep thrusts, as light as those of a snake which glides gently along, or vigorous, like the running of a horse. The woman puts her tongue into the man's mouth, and the bodies melt into each other, in the midst of sucking noises, murmuring and sweat. The man swings his member from one side to the other, and then withdraws it for a moment. He wipes it with a towel and again penetrates right into the very depths. With moaning and groaning noises from both the partners, they follow the instructions of the *Art of the Bedroom*, that is, they alternate short, slow thrusts with other, quicker, deeper ones. The voices of the couple falter, the woman's chignon becomes undone, her comb falls and her hair becomes

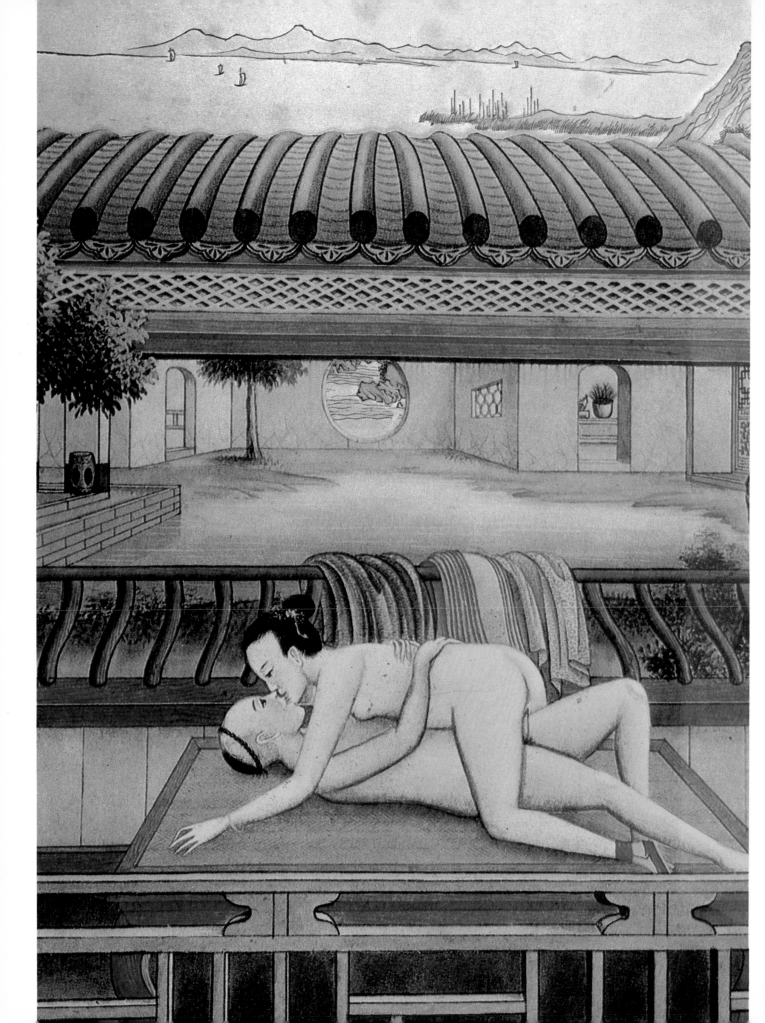

entangled and dishevelled. The man makes movements with his hands and feet, and finally shoots his semen right into the depths of the Vermilion Cavern.

Their bodies and their minds can then relax, and he withdraws his Jade Stem while it is still quite moist. Small droplets exude from the voman's vulva. The maid has prepared perfumed towels, and the two lovers clean themselves with these. They dress themselves again slowly, and adorn themselves with flowers. The woman touches up her make-up. They both smile and give each other light caresses. They adopt their original position again, that is, sitting one beside the other, and their glances are lost in the darkness of night, full of peacefulness and joy, a joy so intense that it will remain for ever engraved in their memories.

The text also gives details concerning the customs of the period. Thus, when it speaks of the Emperor and of his pleasures, it makes it clear that the Empress slept with him for two nights while the moon was full, and that on the other nights, he copulated with nine wives each time. An exact record has been kept of these acts of intercourse, thanks to certain notes which had been made with a paintbrush and red paint. But as the time passed, the situation deteriorated. All the women of the harem, who, in all the different palaces, numbered more than three thousand, tried to show all their charms to the best advantage, in order to become a favourite. This was the source of many cases of jealousy and the harbouring of much resentment. It was only the skill and diplomacy of the Emperor that was able to restore peace and order amongst the wives, and it was certainly no easy task.

The book then gives examples of furtive and illicit affairs, such as in convents, where the nuns were deprived of normal sexual relations. If one can believe the author's version of the story the sisters felt a very strong desire to give themselves to a man, even if they tried not to show it. And it is thus that, when noblemen or important visitors came to their convent, they willingly gave themselves up to the pleasures of sex. Sometimes it also happened that they fell into the arms of unknown monks, especially those who, as was the custom in China, had had their scalp shaved, were tall and vigorous and possessed a penis in proportion to their enormous body. In these cases, the nuns seemed to forget the obligations linked with the law of Buddah completely.

Another kind of romantic adventure took place when a man who happened to be visiting the village tried to creep unnoticed into a woman's room. Sometimes, through fear of being discovered by her husband and being the object of his suspicions, she remained silent and offered no resistance, while another woman might pretend to be asleep and let herself be possessed, enjoying it to the full.

In other circumstances, furtive lovers seized any opportunity that presented itself, that of an assignation or a meeting in some deserted place, for example. Their love-making took place in the forest, in a spot protected from the gaze of onlookers by a wall, on the bank of a river or in the midst of a clump of flowering bushes. Hardly ever did the clandestine lovers enjoy the luxury of having a bed. Their behaviour was that of people who are afraid of being discovered. Their love-making, marked by a feeling of apprehension, lacked the necessary relaxed and peaceful atmosphere. The girl raised the bottom of her clothing and the man lowered his trousers. The union was quickly over, hurried... Certain couples, however, took pleasure in this clandestinity and preferred it, for a time at least, to the peace and quiet of their own room.

"It is necessary to arouse and bring to light feminine feelings, which are sometimes very well hidden and secret. As there are all kinds of women, there is not one single and unique method..."

THE PERFECT UNION: A BATTLE

After the T'ang period, the northern part of China fell into a state of anarchy, while in the south of the country, several emperors followed quickly on each other's heels, their position being especially precarious because of the constant threat of war. In 1226, Gengis Khân dominated the North, while a little later, Qubilai Khân established the capital at Pekin for the first time. The Mongols, however, who were Buddhists, scoffed at the customs and beliefs of the Chinese. In 1368, after nationalist revolts, Chu-Yuan-chang became the first emperor of the Ming dynasty, which ruled over China until 1644, marking the beginning of an age of prosperity, as much in the field of trade and commerce as in the fields of such arts as sculpture and literature.

At this period, it was only the followers of the Tao that were well-informed about sexual methods, and manuals of initiation went through a period of oblivion. At the beginning of the Ming dynasty, however, many works had been reprinted, although only in a limited number of copies. Thus, even the well-educated had little knowledge of the Taoist sexual mystic, so that when they wrote erotic novels or plays they used everyday words, leaving aside the terms of the Taoist vocabulary.

However, there exists a treatise, dating from this period and bearing the title of *True*

Classic of the Perfect Union. Its text is concise and uses the terms of military language, as was frequently the case in these ancient times. It also made use of the Taoist vocabulary. Thus the woman was considered as "the enemy", and the sexual act as "the battle". As the *yin* of the woman was considered as an element indispensable for the vital essence of the man, he was to obtain it without ever losing control of the different phases of the "battle". He must know how to preserve his strength, while taking care to take advantage of the "opponent's" strength and he must also show at first a certain weakness in order to make a better "attack" in due course. This kind of behaviour had its roots in Chinese wrestling and was later to have a great influence on Japanese judo.

The text speaks of a great general, in fact a follower of the Tao, who, at the moment when he was about to enter into contact with the enemy, or to begin his approach to the sexual act, had to concentrate hard, in an attempt to draw the opponent out of her reserve. For that he had to know the plan of campaign of the enemy and to test her sensitivity.

For this purpose, it is necessary to arouse and bring to light feminine feelings, which are sometimes very well hidden and secret. As there are all kinds of women, there is not one single and unique method. Adequate and suitable tactics must then be drawn up and neither cunning nor useful knowledge is to be ignored. To a woman who loves strong drinks, for example, one will give a liqueur to start with. One will converse very tenderly with women of an affectionate nature, one will give very generous presents to those who are greedy and avaricious and one will not hesitate to display one's penis openly in a state of erection to lustful women, in order to excite them.

On the other hand, it will be a matter of taking all kinds of precautions in order not to risk having any unpleasant surprises in the midst of the "battle". To start with, the "warrior" will put out of his mind any idea of lusts of the flesh and will choose a vagina that is fairly wide, so that his own pleasure will be rather slight. The ideal situation is when the woman is ugly or, if this is not the case, one can imagine that she is so in the course of the "struggle"; one will also imagine that she is as unattractive as possible, even odious. The man will introduce his Jade Stem slowly into her, and will then withdraw it again and, having repeated this movement three or four times, he will stop for a moment to allow his desire to calm down. Moreover, at the very moment when the semen is about to flow, he must know perfectly well the art of making it stop and flow back again.

In addition, it is recommended that a man should always carry with him, on any occasion, "a white bandage, boiled in an aphrodisiac substance, and a jade ring", as the great hero Hsi-Men K-ing always did himself. The ring will be placed at the base of the penis and, thanks to the little band it can be attached there by passing the band around one's waist. The ring will generally be carved, and decorated with animal motifs, with dragons, for example, whose tongues curled up in spirals symbolized virility and fertility. These tongues came and caressed, and consequently stimulated, the woman's clitoris.

The man will use all the means at his disposal to "extract" the strength stored up in the "enemy". He will then kiss his partner, will suck her tongue, will caress her breasts and her vulva, will drink in her breath; in short, he will do everything within his powers to arouse her desire.

He himself, the "warrior", will, on the other hand, keep himself as calm and cold as possible during the whole "manoeuvre". He will almost go as far as to show indifference, being in complete control of the situation. In order to do this, he will ensure that his mind, his thoughts, are occupied elsewhere; he will lose himself in the wide open spaces of the heavens, which will enable him to forget his body.

The "enemy", tracked down and harassed, will throw herself into the "battle" with all her vital forces and her passion will flow out of her, leaving her without any means of defence. This is the moment to apply the military tactics of the turtle, the dragon, the snake and the tiger.

"The turtle shuts himself up within himself", which means that, with his eyes and his mouth firmly closed, the man will abstain from touching the woman's body with his feet or his hands; at the same time, he will compress his penis. It is then that "the snake swallows up its prey", which means that the man will kiss the woman, will nibble at her, will suck her, until he has managed to extract from her all her strength, without allowing any of it to escape. "The tiger lies hidden, crouching, ready to attack": the man will remain silent with all, his senses fully alert, trying to restrain his passion. Once the woman will have reached the *ki-ki* point, we arrive at the moment when "the dragon breathes in". This means that the man must take full advantage of the resources of the "enemy" and take possession of the *yin*, by giving brief thrusts alternating with deep ones in a very methodical manner, which will permit him to breath in the secretions. These will rise back up through the spinal column right up to the *Ni-hoan*, which is situated at the very top of the brain.

It is precisely at the moment when the "enemy" is disarmed that one can obtain the victory from which one will reap the richest possible harvest. Then, one will leave the field of battle, will get down from one's battle horse and rest, lying flat on one's back, breathing as calmly and deeply as possible, raising and lowering one's diaphragm, so that the body may take the fullest possible advantage of the "war spoils".

NINE POSITIONS LEADING TO VICTORY

In order to conquer the "enemy", one can, in fact, use any one of the nine positions which, according to the experts, are indispensable if one is to achieve "victory" and the enjoyment of full sexual satisfaction.

As for the first of these positions, it is obtained when the man lies on top of the woman, as she lies on her back. Once the woman has opened her Jade Entrance and the Jade Stem has entered within it with determination, the man begins to move slowly and gives eight slight thrusts and two more powerful ones. The man must introduce his member into the woman before it is completely rigid and, in all the movements that he makes, he must show the extent of his energy and of his joy.

The Walk of the Panther is the name given to the second position. The woman this time kneels down and places her hands on the ground. She raises her buttocks as high as possible and lowers her head. The man, also kneeling behind her, takes hold of the woman's body and penetrates her as deeply as possible with his Jade Stem. He will then perform very rapid movements, alternating short thrusts and longer deeper ones. This is a position which is suitable for curing a great many ills and for increasing one's vigour.

During the Forward Monkey, or the third position proposed, the man takes hold of the woman's legs, as she lies flat on her back, and folds them forwards until the knees reach her breasts. It is at this moment that he inserts his Jade Stem into her. The woman will try to make some movements while the man will do nothing but exert pressure downwards.

In the fourth position the woman lies down on her front, and the man then stretches himself out on top of her. She raises her buttocks as far as possible to create an easier passage for the Jade Stem to enter her. The man will then, once he is inside her, give her six short thrusts, followed by nine deeper ones.

The Rising Tortoise, as the fifth position is called, allows the two partners to begin the pleasures of their love-making gently and smoothly. The woman lies quietly down on her back and raises her legs up high. The man then catches hold of her by the ankles and, still standing upright, places her feet at the same level as his. He thrusts in the Jade Stem in this position and gives her a number of thrusts, sometimes brief ones and sometimes more prolonged ones, according to the rhythm which he considers suitable, and he encourages the movements made by the woman, so that she may achieve a high level of pleasure and satisfaction. This is one of the methods which most increases the strength of the two partners.

To perform the act of love using the sixth position, the woman must stretch herself out

"The manuals of initiation also gave all kinds of advices and explanations concerning procreation. They recommended, for example, that those who want to have a boy, should perform the sexual act on the first or third day after menstruation."

on her back and raise her legs into the air. The man makes as if to sit down backwards on the thighs of his companion, by leaning on the bed with his hands and turning his back towards her. Once he has put the Jade Stem into her, the two partners begin to move, answering each other's cue to continue the movement one after the other. The man, with his buttocks and with his thighs encircles the woman's body. This too is an extremely beneficial position. It can cure all kinds of complaints.

The seventh position is called the Rabbit that Sucks its Fur. The man, in this position, stretches out on his back and it is the woman, in this case, who sits down on him, with her legs spread wide apart, and her knees leaning on the bed. She turns her back on her lover. She will experience a feeling of great joy when the Jade Stem penetrates into her Cavern. Sexual

pleasure and the virility of her partner will disperse all trace of melancholy or nervousness.

The man will lie down on his back again to perform the eighth position. The woman sits on him again too, but this time with her legs stretched out in front of her. He will only introduce the Jade Stem into her very slowly, all the time looking his partner straight in the eyes. As soon as the Jade Stem has entered her, it will remain motionless, while the woman will perform the movements as if she were playing a game. This method is ideal for acquiring a great calmness and peace of mind.

As for the ninth and last position, it is performed like this : the man sits down crosslegged. The woman takes up her position on his crossed legs, and opens her buttocks at the same time as she puts her arms round his neck. The Jade Stem will be inserted as deeply as possible. The two partners will begin to perform movements, swaying backwards and forwards or sideways, according to a rhythm which will suit them both. In order to make things easier, the man will seize hold of the woman's buttocks with both his hands.

If the manuals, in a general way, speak at length about the necessity for making "the

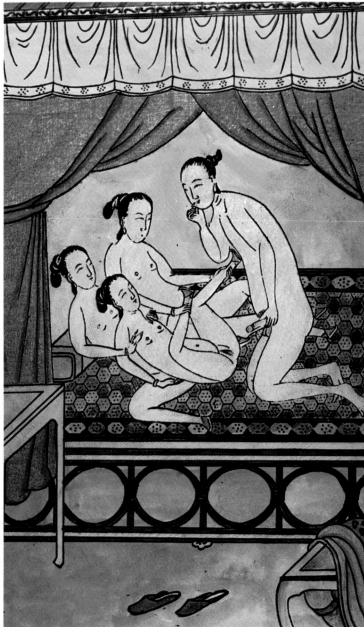

semen return to its source", as well as of the great sexual satisfaction and enjoyment that can be achieved by a woman, if they especially deal with the subject of the return route of the semen "towards the centre of the brain by means of the spinal cord", other books also contain explanations about the "descent" of the semen, in the course of the first phase of the sexual act. This is the case, anyway, of a treatise dating from the Ming period, and produced by a man of letters called Wang Chang-fou. This work explains the difference between the semen which is produced at the time of the sexual act and the primitive or original semen. In fact, it should be one and the same thing. Before sexual desire begins to be aroused, the semen is distributed throughout the whole of the organism through the internal organs and the intestines and it circulates freely without settling in one pre-determined place. This is what is called original semen. But when sexual pleasure begins to have an influence on the organism, the semen starts to make its way down from the centre of the brain to arrive at the bladder, after passing along the spinal cord. At the moment of its discharge, it has become an impure substance.

"One should avoid making love when a rainbow is burning the sky with all the brightness of its colours. A child will cause his parents great unhappiness if he is conceived during the summer or winter solstice."

TALES AND ANECDOTES

The sexual manuals of Ancient China were one source, and a very important source, of inspiration for a certain type of literature of the period, and had an enormous influence on novels and short stories. Their authors revealed in this way that they had a fairly complete and exact knowledge of the Taoist philosophy, or that this philosophy did not leave them completely indifferent, at least as far as its erotic principles were concerned. Thus, it was for example, in the case of Soen Wei, a famous writer of the T'ang period, one of whose tales we are going to tell briefly. He relates the story of an emperor who adored a certain goddess. Once, when one of his most important generals fell ill, he advised him to go and pray in the gardens of his palace, and to address his prayers directly to the famous divinity, requesting her to grant him the favour of a cure. The divinity appeared to the general in the form of a very beautiful young woman, and began to undress herself in front of him, inviting him at the same time to share with her the bliss of the sexual act. The general refused immediately and

firmly. He believed, indeed, that it was his duty to hold himself aloof from any deity. It was not long before the result of his refusal was known. His illness got worse and at the end of a week he died. The goddess came to visit the emperor during his sleep, and explained to him that the general's death was due to the fact that he was lacking in *yang* essence and that if he had agreed to have sexual relations with her, he would still be alive. This story illustrates the theory given in the sex manuals, that declares that the *yin* facilitates the increase of the *yang* during the course of the sexual act.

Other tales take up this anecdote as their theme, introducing some variations. They tell of a love story between a young man and a young woman. Everything happens in a very classic manner, neutral in tone and proper. The young man, full of life, is always getting lost in the forest or on a mountain, after which he manages to find a welcoming house or an inn, where he makes the acquaintance of a young woman. When night falls, the two are joined in love, and the story draws to a happy conclusion. It is usually very short and becomes the pretext for certain scenes of erotism and for descriptions of the sexual act, faithfully following the manuals of initiation in sexual matters.

"Certain women drive into their vagina an ivory penis or a small bag filled with flour, in order to satisfy their desires; old age will be their lot earlier than for their contemporaries."

INITIATION AND PROCREATION

The manuals of initiation also gave all kinds of advice and explanations concerning procreation. They recommended, for example, that those who want to have a boy, should perform the sexual act on the first or third day after menstruation. If, on the other hand, the couple would prefer to have a girl, they should have intercourse on the fourth or fifth day after the woman's period. All the other days of the month were considered as unsuitable for the conception of a child, even when a discharge of semen took place. At the moment of ejaculation, the woman should be lying on her back, so that her heart calm its rapid beat; she should close her eyes and concentrate on her lover's semen.

Lao-Tze, the great Taoist philosopher, claimed that a child would live to an advanced age if he was conceived at midnight. A child conceived before midnight had a good chance of reaching a normal age, whereas a child conceived after this time was likely not to live very long.

A pregnant woman was advised to avoid overwork and strain, as well as conversations

that lasted too long... and they must especially beware of any tension or dispute. She was to concentrate on herself and not attend plays or other entertainments which were inappropriate to her condition, nor make any physical effort, such as that involved in climbing up a steep slope, or walking for too long or too fast, following the edge of a precipice, or riding a horse. It was suggested that she should eat sensibly, not touching raw, cold or too spicy foodstuffs. It would be better for her to avoid as far as possible taking any medicine or other remedies. She should seek at all costs tranquillity and peace of mind. One way of achieving this might be to read the classics out loud. This would tend to make her child good and intelligent. The child's upbringing thus began already before its birth − which is confirmed by the most modern theories − and it was of vital importance to prepare one's child for a happy birth.

In a book on obstetrics, the *Tchan-King,* it is stated that for a human being to be given life, it is essential for the *yin* and the *yang* to become united inside the body of the woman. It is necessary, especially, to adhere to nine important rules so that the child may arrive in the world in the best of conditions. A child must not be conceived during the nine hours of sunshine if one does not want him to suffer frequently from sickness and vomiting. If the child is conceived when the earth and the heavens unite their elements on a neutral site, he will be either deaf or blind. One must also abstain from sexual intercourse with a discharge of semen during an eclipse of the sun, for a child conceived at this time will die as a result of injuries of

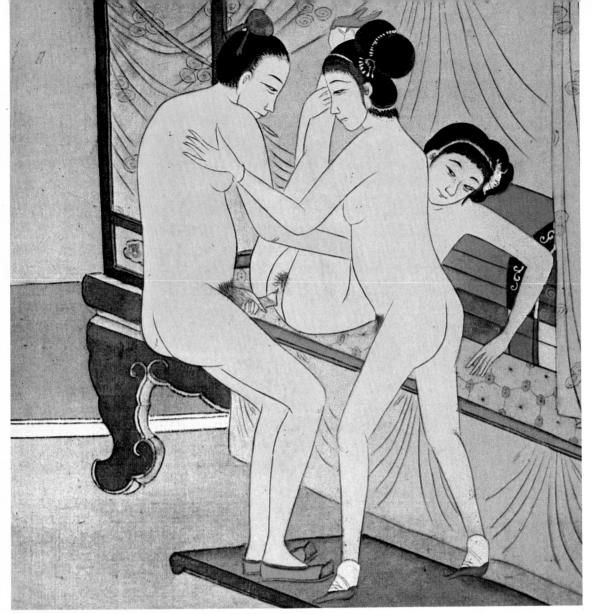

"From 618 to 907, China was governed by the T'ang dynasty. During this period arts and sciences reached their zenit, and it was also at this time that manuals about sex became commonplace and easily laid hands on" (left).

"The Vigorous Peak inspects the whole of the back of the cavern with brief thrusts, sometimes with a rotating movement... Sou-nu has given a name to each part of the external sexual organs of the woman: two centimetres inside, one finds the Lute String; at twelve centimetres the Wheat Seed."

some kind or of burns. A child conceived during a storm, in the midst of flashes of lightning and claps of thunder, would risk being mentally handicapped. An eclipse of the moon could only have a harmful influence on the child, and would ring misfortune upon him, and for the same reason one should avoid making love when a rainbow is burning the sky with all the brightness of its colours. A child will cause his parents great unhappiness if he is conceived during the summer or winter solstice. He will be killed in a war if the parents copulate during a night when the moon is full. He will become epileptic and his body will break out into a rash of ulcers if he is conceived after a great banquet, or if his parents are in a state of drunkenness.

The weather conditions can also have a considerable influence on the state of the future child. Thus the Daughter of Candour suggests that one should purify one's heart, forget all one's troubles and problems, make very slow, dignified movements, maintain one's body in a relaxed state, and rid one's thoughts of all evil ideas by means of fasting, before thinking of copulating to give life to a new human being. During the days which follow the woman's menstruation, during the night and before the cock crows for the first time, the man will arouse the woman to the delights of sexual pleasure. When the two partners both feel in harmony with each other, they will make love with the purest of joy. This is the only way of obtaining a child who is both wise and good.

Pong-Tsu adds that the man will avoid discharging his semen for several days, so that at the moment of coition the semen will be abundant and will facilitate conception. This condition will enable the child to take possession of the wisdom which is his due, to have talent and a remarkable position in life, if it is a boy, or to be pure, wise, beautiful and blessed with tenderness and generosity if it is a girl. And when they are born, during a change of season or of moon the boy's foreskin will open and reveal the glans, while the girl's lips will expand. With the passing of the years the young pubes will become covered with hair, and the "red liquid" will flow from the female body. Little by little, both boy and girl will have reached their state of maturity and will soon have to choose a wife or a husband in their turn. They will exchange presents with their heart's choice, and one day they will get married. Then the night will come for them, with its promise of sexual pleasure and enjoyment. They will learn the different positions, the suitable movements, the slow or rapid thrusting, the whispering, the caresses, the kisses and all that is necessary for the harmony of the *yin* and the *yang*.

BENEFICIAL FEMALE SECRETIONS

Both the man and the woman will take care not to fall into the clutches of debauchery, the source of all kinds of illnesses. In any case, let them not forget that complaints caused by the sexual act can also be cured by it, as one can cure someone of drunkenness by prescribing alcoholic drinks for him. To improve her sight, for example, the woman will raise her head and hold her breath at the moment when the man's semen is released. She will be careful not to waste any of it. Contracting the muscles of her stomach, and driving out her wrath by the brightness of her pupils, she will allow the semen to reach right into the deeply hidden depths of the veins, and thus will recover her lost health.

A treatise which was very well-known during the period of the Ming dynasty, had even made an inventory of the beneficial properties of the female secretions. This text, which

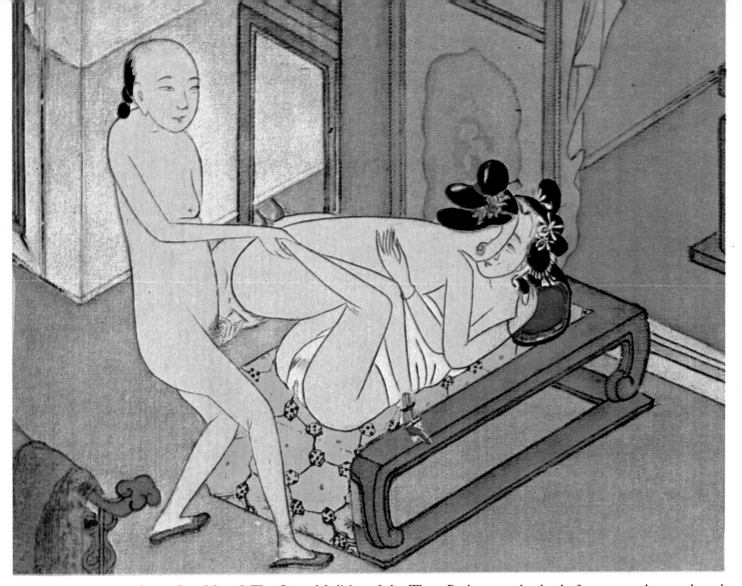

bore the title of *The Great Medicine of the Three Peaks,* was the basis for an erotic novel and inspired a number of other pieces, mainly poetry.

The names of the three peaks are the following: the Peak of the Red Lotus, the Peak of the Double Lotus and the Peak of the Purple Agaric.

The Peak of the Red Lotus is the highest of the three; its medicine is called the Jade Fountain, the Jade Fluid or the Fountain of the Sweet Spirits. It is grey in colour and its source is to be found in the two cavities situated under the woman's tongue. When it flows out of the Flowery Field, the man must swallow it in such a way that it reaches the Pagoda with several floors, and is collected into his Vermilion Field. His five internal organs will benefit by being well moistened, the Mysterious Doorway on the left will be fortified, and the Vermilion Field on the right will be enlarged. In addition, the production of vital essence and new blood will be stimulated.

The second peak, the Peak of the Double Lotus is of medium height. Its medicine is the fruit of Immortality, also called the Whiteness of Snow, because of its white colour, or Coral Juice, perhaps because of its pleasantly sweet taste. The source of this remedy is to be found in a woman's two breasts. The man has to sip it and swallow it. Once the medicine has been collected in his Vermillon Field, it will nourish both his spleen and his stomach, and will also help the circulation of the blood in the woman whose medicine has been sucked out, and will fill her body and soul with a joyous feeling of sexual pleasure. All the humours of her body will be displayed, and will increase as it reaches right up to the Flowery Waters and right down to the Mysterious Doorway. The second peak is the one to which one should give

"It is absolutely necessary for the two partners to be in complete accord in the sexual act."

one's attention in the first place. If the woman has not yet borne a child, and thus has no milk in her breasts, the results will be even more beneficial.

The Peak of the Purple Agaric, the lowest peak of the three, is also called the Cave of the Wild Beast, or the Mysterious Gateway. Its medicine is called the Heavy White Metal or the Flower of the Moon. It takes its source from the very depths of the vagina. Although its door is normally closed, when the act of coition rouses the woman to sexual pleasure, a blush will come to her cheeks, her voice will falter and fade away, then the door opens and out will flow an abundant secretion of liquid at the very moment when the woman reaches the topmost height of her enjoyment.

To nourish his spirit, the man must take advantage of the *original yang,* and draw his member back towards him as soon as the liquid has collected in the woman's vagina. After inching his penis slowly away, he will then thrust it forwards and backwards again, in order to pump the woman's essence.

RECIPES FOR REDISCOVERING YOUTH OR INCREASING VIRILITY

The sexual medicine of Ancient China offered, then, remedies for all kinds of troubles and disorders when it was not simply a matter of keeping or consolidating a health that was already in fairly good condition. Medicaments existed capable of encouraging the

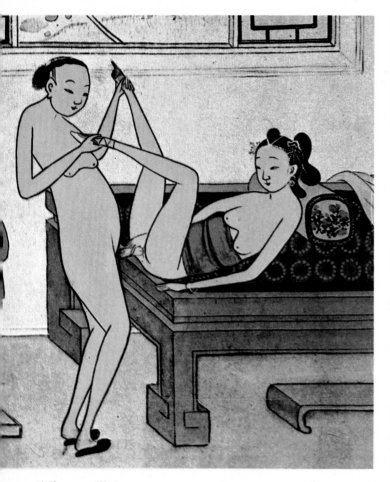

"There will be caresses, sweet murmurs, embraces and kisses, with lips against lips and body against body, each of the couple gorging himself or herself on the saliva of the other. The man will nibble the lips or the tongue of his partner a little."

development of a man's penis, or of bringing about the contraction of a vagina that was too broad, or of curing the bleeding resulting from a woman's deflowering, or of soothing pain, diminishing the virility of a man or turning him into a eunuch, relieving the discomfort felt in the vagina after or during the sexual union, driving away headaches, healing a debilitating weakness or impotence, amongst other things.

Certain prescribed advice had come to be of great importance in sexual manuals and in medical treatises. One of the pieces of advice, for example, described how to increase a man's virility. It was said that a woman had given it to her slave before it was dictated in public during the course of a trial. This is what has to be done: Take ten grammes of a powder made from a stem of *Rehmannia lutea,* cut very fine, which one will soak in an alcoholic drink, with two grammes of cinnamon, two grammes of *Atractylis ovata,* five grammes of *Kan-tsi* and five grammes of *Kan-tsau* or *Glycyrrhiza glabra.* This powder, thus made up of five ingredients, should be taken three times a day after meals in a spoonful of some alcoholic beverage.

To find out what the effects might be, let us follow the story of the woman through whom this recipe was first made known. Her husband, who was already eighty years old at the time, had himself prepared this concoction, in the hope of rediscovering his virility. But he died without having been able to take the powder. So the woman made a present of it to one of her slaves, who was himself already aged seventy. He had white hair, walked very slowly and his body was completely bent and twisted. He took the potion regularly for twenty days, and his body gradually straightened. To the great surprise of everyone, his hair recovered its

beautiful original black colour, and his skin its smoothness and its healthy glow. One would have thought him to be thirty years old. The woman, who also had two women servants, offered them to the man as a present, in order to make his happiness complete. He produced several children by them. Then one evening while the slave was drunk and was looking for another woman, rather than his own, to make love to, his mistress gave herself to him out of curiosity. She then experienced, in spite of her fifty years, a desire so strong at his very touch, and a pleasure so violent that she could not bring herself to let the man go. Never before had she experienced anything of this kind. Her life was completely changed by it, and after that, she shared the slave in question with her two women servants. They lived together, holding a ceaseless sexual orgy. What better proof could be given of the effectiveness of the powder that the slave had taken!

Another recipe, ideal, so it seems, for maintaining virility and curing all one's disorders, is called the remedy of the Bald Chicken. It consists of grinding to powder a mixture of three grammes of each of the following ingredients: *Boschinakia glabra, Schizandra sinensis, Cuscuta japonica, Polygala japonica* and *Cridium japonicum*. This powder should be taken on an empty stomach, mixed with a tablespoonful of wine. The manuals state that if one continues to take it over a period of sixty days, one will be able to copulate with more than forty woman. At the beginning and during the first nine days, they recommend that it should be taken three times a day. Its name of "Bald Chicken" recalls its origins. The man who invented it, in fact, the Prefect Taking brought the following misadventure upon himself. He worked out the recipe for this mixture when he was seventy years old and took it regularly. At the end of a short time, he felt such a strong desire to copulate that he decided to interrupt the treatment and threw the rest of the mixture away in the courtyard. A cock swallowed it.Immediately, he was seized by such a frenzy that he mounted a hen, and did not let her out of his sight for several days. In his pleasure in his sexual powers, temporarily increased in this way, he pecked at her head until she was completely bald!

There is a cream that encourages the growth of a penis considered to be too small. The basic ingredients: a powder made up of three grammes of *Boschinakia glabra* and two grammes of glasswort, mixed with part of the liver of a white dog killed when the moon is new. This should be spread on the penis three times a day and washed off with fresh water at the end of a period of two or three hours.

To cure frigidity in a woman and to make her vagina more supple, a powder should be concocted using two grammes of sulphur, two grammes of *Inula incense,* a little *Cidrium japonicum* and just a few grains of *Evodia rutaecarpa*. Small quantities of the mixture should be inserted into the vagina before each sexual act. It should not, however, be used too frequently, as this may lead to a complete closure of the vaginal opening.

Another very simple recipe for bringing about the contraction of the vagina is to mix three parts of sulphur in one part of warm water.

Finally, a last recipe, which can be used in a large number of cases: it can encourage the member to erect at the touch of a woman's body, it can cure debility, and combat pains in the regions of the waist or back. The day to use it is to take after each meal a small spoonful of a powder composed of crushed deer horn, cedar seeds, *cuscuta japonica, plantago, polygala japonica* and *Boschniakia glabra,* mixed together in equal quantities.